DATE DUE

MAR 1 5 '95			
AUG 1 4 2000			

Basic Money

Managing Personal Finances on Your Microcomputer

Basic Money

Managing Personal Finances on Your Microcomputer

Charles Seiter

▲
▼▼
Addison-Wesley Publishing Company
Reading, Massachusetts   Menlo Park, California
London   Amsterdam   Don Mills, Ontario   Sydney

Copyright © 1984 by Addison-Wesley Publishing Company, Inc.

Library of Congress Cataloging in Publication Data

Seiter, Charles.
  Basic Money.

  Includes index.
  1. Finance, Personal—Data processing. 2. Basic
(Computer program language) I. Title.
HG179.S4 1984   332.024'00285425   83–21385
ISBN 0–201–06599–1

Cover design by Marshall Henrichs. Text design by Lori Snell.
Set in 11-point Aster by Kingsport Press.

ISBN 0–201–06599–1

ABCDEFGHIJ–DO–87654

Contents

Basic Money

Managing Personal Finances
on Your Microcomputer

INTRODUCTION
What to Do
with a Computer

This book is intended for adults with no previous experience in computing. Specifically, it is aimed at people who have found themselves in possession of a computer, probably because it was an irresistible bargain at its price, and are now wondering what to do with it.

The small computer is an interesting product, mainly because it is difficult to believe that something so cheap and so readily available (the author lives in a town of 3,000 people and could easily buy six kinds of small computers from various stores) could be a real computer. Well, it is, and used properly it can help you do the kind of financial computation you used to have to trust your bank to do.

The reason for the emphasis on financial computation is twofold:

- What adults need computers for is money management, not games.
- Small computers are very good at this work.

All these computers will accommodate different levels of expansion, from added RAM to disk drives to printer interfaces. An enormous amount of valuable work can be done with these systems right as they come out of the box, with no added memory and just the usual provision for cassette recording. The trick is in writing programs that are compact enough to type in easily, with clean and simple output that can be copied right off the screen. The programs in this book can all be entered in a few minutes each and saved on cassette tape. This is what this book has to recommend itself to you: you may not need to do word processing or spreadsheet calculation, and for that matter the smallest computers are not so hot at these applications anyway, but you probably do have a credit card or a savings account or a mortgage, and in figuring your real costs in these connections, *any* computer is just wonderful.

As you read through this book (and it should be possible just to read through and not work through), you will probably acquire an intuitive appreciation of several facts of life:

IN MONEY
- what inflation can do to you in twenty years
- what difference it will make to you if an expense is tax-deductible
- how much money you will pay out in interest in the course of your life

IN COMPUTERS
- how big (or small) 1K RAM is
- what you would do with a disk drive or a printer
- what a tremendous lot of computing power you can get for a small amount of money

There are three parts to this book. The first part contains an overview of current (mid-1980s) economic conditions, and presents a review of the small part of the BASIC language that is used in the programs. The second part contains four chapters on specific topics; if you know some BASIC or have done the examples in your computer manual, you may as well pick out a topic you find interesting and plunge right in. The third part is something of a postscript, and presents a simple version of a model of investment prices, we hope with some practical conclusions. Many very practical results appear with just a little bit of computing!

1
What Has Happened to Your Money

This book is addressed to a particular audience, an audience that, however, includes most working adult Americans. It is concerned with people whose economic activity consists mostly of working for a regular paycheck and distributing their funds in regular monthly payments. The reason that these people (is this you?) could stand a little help is that inflation and problems with the American taxation and retirement pension systems have taken, in the last fifteen years, a dreadful toll on their finances.

An odd feature of the finances of most people locked into the monthly paycheck vs. monthly bills situation is that little attention is given to the expense of the major purchase in the budget, which is not *stuff* but *money*! At the end of thirty years of $1,000-a-month mortgage payments on a $95,000 house, John Doe has spent $360,000; the price of the house is really a small part of what old John has bought with his life's earnings; mostly he has bought the use of other people's money. Clearly, it becomes very important to study one's finances in the light of loan costs and the tax situations that arise from them.

One of the problems confronting people who would like to do something about their financial situation is that all decisions nowadays have to be undertaken with accurate information about the "time value of money." This means that people should be able to figure the impact of payments on money borrowed at interest and also to calculate what is happening to their money as a result of inflation. For all practical purposes, these computations cannot be done by hand and require a good deal of attention to execute on a calculator with financial function keys.

Fortunately, this sort of work is pleasantly and easily carried out on even the smallest computers with a video display. No knowledge of programming is required (although a lot may be acquired by watching the programs), and the information is collected and answers presented in a clear and readable way.

This chapter won't contain any actual programming (and don't worry anyway; the programming will be nice and simple when it does appear) but will show the results of calculations on different money situations. First, there is a section on the impact of inflation on average people; unless you are a really hardened character, you should find this more horrifying than a low-budget ax-murder movie. Second, there is a somewhat discouraging review of the prospects of the typical IRA account and the idea of retirement savings in general. Then there is a detailed example of the results of buying vs. renting in real estate, offered as a sort of dim light at the end of the tunnel.

These cases will be seen later in the book to have emerged from very simple computer programs, really just the next step up from the kind of thing that can be done on a programmable financial calculator. Curiously, the least expensive computers (e.g., Timex, VIC 20, TI 99/4A) are now cheaper than fancy calculators and will easily pay for themselves the first time you figure out auto financing with them.

Where You Stand:
Inflation vs. Income

We may as well plunge into the worst news first. For your consideration, here are four studies of the consequences of inflation, taken from statistical studies on wage earners in different income categories. You may find yourself somewhere in these examples, and if you do, it will probably explain why you may feel you are running very hard to stay in the same place.

EXAMPLE
John and Jane Workhard

We will suppose that John and Jane have slogged through the last fifteen years at roughly the same jobs. Jane was making $6,000 a year as a relatively well-paid secretary in 1967, and John was raking in the big bucks, i.e., $14,000 per year, as an attorney a few years out of law school. That year they paid $3,210 in taxes and bought a new Porsche. As we look in on them in 1982, Jane has gotten regular raises and is now making $11,000 per year, and John is now bringing home $31,000. This example is presented with no imagination cranked in at all—the pay raises are from government average statistics. Now watch this little comparison, and we'll see why they reminisce a lot about the good old days:

	Income	Taxes	Net
1967	$20,000	$3,210	$16,780
1982	$42,000	$9,985	$32,115
1982 net in 1967 dollars =	$32,115/2.8 = $11,470		

Basically, after fifteen years of hard work and regular pay raises, the Workhards have lost enough ground to drop into a lower socioeconomic class than they were in when they were fresh out of college. Hmmm . . . no Porsche this year, and very likely not even a new Toyota.

EXAMPLE
Professor Diligence

A truly interesting example of virtue rewarded may be drawn from academic life, a sphere of endeavor in which spiritual rewards have recently greatly outweighed material ones. To a certain extent this is the result of a trend in population statistics: about twenty years ago, having babies fell sharply out of fashion and college enrollments will be dropping all through the 1980s.

Professor Diligence was a postdoctoral fellow in 1967 (this is what you do between your Ph.D. and your first major-league academic job) earning a prestigious $11,500, and his wife, Judy Diligence, was bringing in $4,500 from an office job at the same university. Because of the tax laws on fellowships, they paid $1,200 in income taxes.

Fifteen years later, Professor Diligence has worked so steadily at his craft, publishing, researching, and teaching, that he has been promoted to Full Professor. Judy Diligence got disgusted with him for working nights and weekends and holidays, and checked out in 1979 for a pottery collective north of San Francisco. Professor Diligence now earns $26,500 and is living with one of his graduate students, but filing a single return devoid of such reactionary claptrap as interest deductions on a mortgage. The professor's relative financial situation looks like this:

	Income	Taxes	Net
1967	$16,000	$1,200	$14,800
1982	$26,500	$5,896	$20,604
1982 net in 1967 dollars =	$20,604/2.8 = $ 7,358		

This interesting case derives both from the Bureau of Labor Statistics wage tables and the divorce rate among younger college faculty members. In a more sentimental scenario, if Judy Diligence were to return home and get remarried to the professor, her $10,000 annual income added to his would leave them with $10,200 1967 dollars after taxes. This is a hard game to win, and leaves the professor open to the horrid American question, "If he's so smart, why ain't he rich?"

The driving force in this strange situation is the fact that the tax tables haven't been seriously modified in a long time. You are now being paid in funny money, whereas in 1967 you were being paid in rather large dollars (they were worth 4 German marks instead of 2.3 or so). A quick look at these summary tables underlines this point:

TAXES THEN AND NOW

Income	Tax 1967	1982
$20,000	$3,100	$2,900
$30,000	$5,600	$5,600
$40,000	$9,400	$9,200

So that you would have the same real disposable income after taxes from the same starting income, the rates for the upper brackets should be less than half what they are now. In other words, with $30,000 per year in 1967, you were rather well-off; in 1982, you're just slightly better than average but are still in the "rich folks" tax bracket. Neat, eh? (The tables above are an approximation for a two-person joint return.)

EXAMPLE
Randy Success

Randy Success will be an example of a hard-charging young go-getter who is actually making more money in 1982 than he was in 1967. In 1967 Randy took a job as a flunky in a West Coast recording studio. Finding that most of the work involved finding recreational pharmaceuticals for musicians late at night, he took a job bartending in the afternoons to supplement his income and expand his potential utility to the studio (we are not at liberty to divulge details here). For 1967, Randy took in $11,000 and paid $1,050 in taxes (some income items were in cash, and forgetful young Randy neglected to include them on his 1040 form, resulting in about $400 tax savings).

Well, our plucky young hero plunged ahead and did what was necessary to succeed in the recording industry in Hollywood. Since all computer books are rated PG, you will have to use your imagination to fill in the career path, but it can be disclosed that he is now being paid $96,000 a year as a top executive and has just dozens of sincere friends. The record company he works for has suffered from IRS scrutiny in the matter of executive compensation, so his income is all reported (ouch!) on a proper W-2. Let's see how this works out:

	Income	Taxes	Net
1967	$10,500	$ 1,050	$ 9,450
1982	$96,000	$39,318	$56,682

1982 net in 1967 dollars = $56,682/2.8 = $20,243

What our hero's exertions amount to is that he is making about twice as much real money as he was fifteen years ago tending bar and running errands. He could help himself out somewhat by buying a house instead of leasing a red-hot condo in Westwood, but the poor guy has never scraped together a down payment, what with the upkeep on his gold chains and all.

This example is meant mostly to illustrate what amazing amounts of money are required simply to double one's income in fifteen years, something that would have been thought of as a goal so modest as to be taken for granted by most enterprising young fellows in the late 1960s. Getting ahead is going to require some calculation.

EXAMPLE
Ed and Cindy Mittel

Ed and Cindy are representative of the people who do a great deal of the hard work in this society and are not especially well paid for it. Ed was driving a truck for $4.00 an hour in 1967 (a little better than truck-driving average) and Cindy was getting $2.30 an hour sewing swimsuits. Fifteen years later, Ed makes $9.40 an hour and Cindy makes $4.50. We can just run this up conveniently and see how the relentless march of progress has dealt with the Mittels.

	Income	Taxes	Net
1967	$13,000	$1,800	$11,200
1982	$31,000	$5,950	$25,050
1982 net in 1967 dollars =		$25,050/2.8 = $ 8,946	

This is not faring quite as badly as some other examples, but it is a showpiece example of the effects of taxation "bracket creep" on middle-income families (the Mittels here are doing better than average, according to the tables). The occupations of truck driver and sewing-machine operator were chosen because truckers' salaries have outpaced inflation somewhat, while apparel workers' have lagged slightly. On straight salary, the Mittels should be fairly close to even with inflation; their problem is that *they are in a higher tax bracket, but not making more real money.* It is this effect that is reducing the purchasing power of millions of average families, and there is every reason to believe it will become more severe. In the Mittels' case, the effect of this tax problem is a loss to them of about $3,000 a year in 1982 money (or $1,000 in 1967 dollars). This hurts, and it hurts a lot; it is about 10% of their income.

A computer book is perhaps an odd place for a political statement, but it is really astonishing how little serious complaint is raised about this situation. Perhaps we should all be comforted that Americans are so docile and agreeable in the face of adversity. Perhaps it is just that people have a hard time mobilizing their anger over a very gradual drift into poverty as opposed to a sudden catastrophe. In any case, a primary aim of this book is to enable you to form a clear picture, in numbers rather than vague impressions, or what is happening to your money. The peculiar linkage of taxation tables and inflation makes a truly distressing mechanism to contemplate. In an attempt to correct this, or at least freeze the tables at their current wildly unacceptable level of injustice, legislation was passed in the early 1980s that "indexes" tax tables to the consumer price index. While this is at least a hopeful step, there are two problems with it that won't go away. First, the repeal of these bills is already being argued vigorously in the face of rising government deficits; at some point the indexing scheme will have to be modified or the federal government will be soaking up the entire capital market. Second, the consumer price index, to which the scheme has been linked, has frequently been tampered with for political reasons and is fairly likely to be tampered with again. Thus the bracket-creep problem, while supposedly slowed down for the moment, is always going to be a very difficult consequence of inflation to manage.

Golden Years:
Second Thoughts about the IRA Program

An exceptionally interesting type of calculation is figuring retirement benefits. Actually, this sort of work at first would appear to be one of the most boring activities on earth, but it turns out to be a confirmation of a discovery about human behavior that has implications in gambling theory and many other psychological/mathematical endeavors. The discovery is simple: given a payoff schedule, a set of probabilities, and choices to make, people in general grossly underestimate the possibility of disaster and greatly overestimate the possibility of small winnings. This is why people invariably love to play supermarket contests and enter drawings (*5000 Third Prizes of $25 Each!!!*), but are reluctant to check the oil in their automobiles until their engines seize. Have you ever won third prize in a supermarket contest? On the other hand, have you ever run out of gas, in a car with a perfectly good gas gauge, in fact driving past gas stations to do it? This strange internal biasing of probabilities is one of the most consistent features of human personality (the author at this point is not trying to pretend to be omniscient, and on the contrary is a textbook example of this failing!).

Just this quirk of human behavior appears to be at work in the unbridled enthusiasm for the individual retirement account, familiarly known as the IRA. It is reliably reported that almost seven million IRAs were opened in March/April 1983, resulting in an absolutely delirious flood of long-term deposits to happy banks and savings-and-loans. There is no question that the people doing this expect some remarkable benefits from their acts of fiscal prudence, and that these benefits, being far in the future, are viewed somewhat optimistically.

As a sample of the kind of computing power available in your computer, the results of a very simple twelve-line program will be presented. The details of programming appear in the next chapter, and the considerations involved in savings accounts and retirement plans are covered in chapter 6. The key point here is to see what the computer, which has neither hopes nor fears, thinks of a typical IRA.

EXAMPLE
Those Swinging Sunset Years

Arthur Thrift at age thirty begins putting $2,000 per year into an IRA at a bank. The bank is paying 11% as he starts this amazingly regular practice, and he expects that something like this interest level will be maintained throughout the whole thirty-five years until he plans to draw on it (it might be noted that there is no historical basis whatsoever for this belief, but we will go with this cheerful assumption for now).

It is a simple matter of compounding to figure how much is in the account when Arthur is sixty-five:

```
CASE 1: Interest = 11%
        Inflation = 0%
        Total = $683,179
        Real  = $683,179
```

This distinction between *total* and *real* will be clear when an inflation rate other than zero is used; at zero inflation here it means that these dollars are of the same value as those Arthur started with in 1983.

There is already a tiny hint of trouble in paradise.

We don't know what Arthur's tax bracket will be in 2018 when he begins drawing on the account. If he budgets the money to last ten to twelve years or so, he is in the 50% bracket by 1983 standards. One of the premises suggested at the founding of the IRA program was that the government will certainly have lowered the tax rates by the time current IRA savers are retiring. This is a matter for faith rather than computation, and the reader is encouraged to search his own memory for examples of massive tax reduction. Now please stop laughing long enough to read the next case.

CASE 2: Interest = 11%
          Inflation = 10.4% (the 1981 actual rate)
          Total = $683,179
          Real = $77,634

This is the serious hint that something can go wrong with an IRA, and as you might expect what can go wrong is inflation. Arthur now retires and begins paying himself $60,000 per year. This puts him in the 50% tax bracket in the eyes of the government circa 1983. However, what poor old Arthur (and poor and old are going to look pretty accurate in a minute) is really doing is paying himself $7,000 per year, in constant 1983 dollars, but the government is now going to want a nice chunk (half, if the rules don't change) of what they see as his princely income.

What has happened here is that, if the inflation rate is very close to the interest rate, Arthur is just going to get back his original thirty-five years times $2,000, which is exactly $70,000. What is also evident here is the mechanism that can ultimately bring down *any* retirement scheme, namely, inflation. All the old dollars the workers in the Depression put into Social Security are now worth less than a fifth of their original value, and no one would be able to retire if Social Security and many other pension plans were not actually financed out of current revenues.

It might be remarked before we proceed to the next case that numerous respected financial observers have suggested that the IRA is a scheme to allow the individual taxpayer to find himself in the same trouble as Social Security itself. The taxpayer, however, can't print money nor can he tax anyone else. The government and the banks contend that the IRA is a wonderful tax shelter for the average person, or at least a wonderful tax deferment. Decisions, decisions. This most primitive version of an IRA calculation is not taking into account the cumulative impact of your modest tax savings over the years (the broad conclusion still stands in general). Furthermore, if you can contrive to drop dead before retirement, there are benefits for your estate in an IRA. But for now we shall play this game straight and see what's in it for you.

CASE 3: Interest = 11%
        Inflation = 8%
        Total = $683,179
        Real = $120,924

A fairly reasonable assumption is that interest rates, being managed in each country by that country's central bank, will run a few points higher than the inflation rate. There is historical evidence for this belief. To see what has happened to Arthur's account, we will also project that the tax tables have been slashed in half in a series of sweeping reforms (a little optimism may be allowable; after all, we are already assuming that Arthur and his bank are not radioactive dust). Under these conditions, we find Arthur at age sixty-five, paying himself $60,000 per year, giving $15,000 in taxes to the government, and finding himself with an actual $7,900 (after taking inflation into account, in 1983 dollars) to live on in his sunset years. If the tax cut never arrives, he will only have $5,300.

    A still more gruesome and touchy problem is that the banks' position is that they have to quote an interest rate higher than the inflation rate in order to attract deposits. But in a remarkable coincidence of interests, both the government and the banks thus find it in their interest to come up with an inflation figure that may in fact be modest compared to the real one. During the year this book was written, the official U.S. government figure was quoted as about 3.5%. While this had the wonderful effect of giving the government a modest burden for cost-of-living raises to various of its dependents, the figure 3.5% was persistently quoted in foreign financial journals as a source of light amusement (independent foreign economists saw the U.S. rate for the same period as 6 to 8%, depending on index design).

The tax question and the inflation rate therefore decide whether an IRA will pay off or not. In a high-inflation model, it is just a mechanism for generating lots of tax. In a moderate inflation model, it might actually provide a pensioner with enough to have an apartment and fend off starvation. If the inflation rate goes above the interest rate for any length of time, Arthur is absolutely wiped out (we'll save that case for chapter 6). In fairness to the IRA concept, if you know something about investments and can manage an *active* IRA full of stock deals and other shenanigans, you may well be able get ahead of the inflation rate and have a small fortune when you retire. Then if the government lets you keep it (taxes again!), you have beaten the system at last. Just don't count on a straight bank-account IRA to produce the same results.

A Ray of Hope

The beleaguered folks whose cases have been described in this chapter have approximately one hope of doing something about their condition, a hope sanctioned in tax laws written back during the Depression. It happens that making interest payments on home mortgages tax-deductible appeared to be one of the few ways the government could attempt to prevent millions of people from being evicted from their homes. Thus the interest on home payments is tax-deductible; in an extension of this principle that most other nations find bizarre, *all* interest payments are deductible. This has given the United States about the lowest personal savings rate of any industrial nation, and it also means that in this country, if you are renting property instead of buying, you are someone else's answer to inflation and someone else's retirement plan.

A few simple illustrations can be worked up with the

aid of a miniature tax table (later this sort of thing will be incorporated into a program in the chapter on housing). We will consider two cases, first that of Joe Single and next that of John and Emily McNormal.

Joe Single is looking at the tax tables for filing in 1983 and confronts the following discouraging information:

Income	Tax
$50,000	$16,306
$40,000	$11,419
$30,000	$ 7,182

On a lazy Sunday morning, Joe is sitting in his $700 per month apartment, wondering idly why he is broke all the time. He is glancing, uncharacteristically, at real-estate ads for lovely garden condominiums but notes with dismay that the monthly payments would be $833 per month and is not sure how that would work out (that's what this book is about—he won't have to wonder anymore if he buys a small computer). It happens that Joe makes $40,000 per year and for all practical purposes has no deductions, putting him up for the abovementioned $11,419. If he were making condo payments, he would have, for the first few years, a deduction of $10,000, giving him a taxable income of $30,000 and taxes of $7,182. This means that he shells out $10,000 in payments but gets a tax break of $4,237. Effectively, his monthly payments in the condo are about $480 per month. And that, dear reader, is the way it all works under the laws of this republic as currently constituted. Everybody knows this or has heard something about it, but it helps to have the consequences put in exact numbers. (Question: who gets the tax break on the financing in Joe's current apartment? Right! Tax laws tend to favor the people with down-payment money.)

The McNormals' situation is similar, but last year they borrowed a down payment from Emily's parents, the Averages, and are now making $1,000-per-month payments on a v. cln. 2BR/2bath fixer-upper in a reasonable suburb.

They make $50,000 between them, and it works out that their payments drop them from taxes of $13,294 to $8,425 (it's not just the deduction per se—it's that they end up in a much lower bracket). The upshot of this is that their real monthly cost of housing is $595 instead of $1,000. This is the kind of government subsidy people associate with tobacco farmers, not suburbanites.

This situation works as well at lower income levels from a tax standpoint; the only problem at lower income levels is finding property you can afford, given the fairly ruinous real-estate inflation of the last ten years. Later in this book, a comparison of the effects of dumping $2,000 per year into an IRA versus sending it to the bank on a mortgage payment are compared. Very interesting.

Now if you know nothing about computers at all, you should proceed to chapter 2. If you have worked through the manual that came with the computer, you should have no trouble picking out a chapter with a problem that interests you and running the programs with no further ado. If you already know everything about everything, read the chapter on speculation; it has some material that qualifies it as light computer entertainment, and may provoke you to write some more advanced programs yourself. Good luck and have fun!

2
First Steps

One of the delightful surprises awaiting you here is that the amount of programming you have to know to get some use out of this book is exactly zero. That is, the programs have already been written, are very short, and all you have to do is type them in. You will also find, as you go through a few chapters, that much *less* is going on here in the BASIC language than you might think from looking through your computer manual. The baby-sized version of BASIC used in this book has pretty much eliminated all the nifty nonstandard features of the language that have been developed for different computers. There are thus about twenty small computers on the market in the mid-1980s that will run all of these programs with no modifications required.

So the good news is that you don't have to know much to get going in this material and perhaps save yourself some money on your finances. The bad news is that that's *all* you're going to be able to impress people with at parties—you won't necessarily know enough about computers or BASIC or high-tech nonsense to impress anyone over the age of six. As a consolation here, the author humbly suggests that the extra money you can save will do you some good, whereas gossip about particular computers or programming languages is rather perishable.

If you have diligently studied your computer manual, you may skip the next few sections and plunge into the real programs. If, on the other hand, you have forgotten most of the manual or have never read it in the first place, the following exercises will get you up to the "programming" level you need to get useful results from this book.

Cold Start

Turn on the computer and connect it to a television or monitor according to the setup instructions in the manual. You should see some sort of indication on the screen (a little blinking underline symbol, or perhaps a little blinking square, called a *cursor*) that the computer is ready to start work. If it comes up with a few lines of script, this might be a good time to rummage through the manual and see if you have an instruction such as CLEAR or CLR to clear the screen. If you are using one of the smaller machines with BASIC built in, most of the steps to follow will be pretty simple. In some disk-based BASICs, you may have to come up with a file name before you start work (owning such a machine already brands you as a swinger and it will be assumed you know your way around a keyboard).

Now type in the number 1984, just as you would on a calculator, and then RETURN (or on some machines, ENTER). You should see the number on the screen, and the blinking cursor beneath or beside it, waiting to give you another shot. So far so good.

The Uses of "Print"

Let's print something, at least in the peculiar sense of printing something on a television screen (you will see later that none of the programs in this book calls for real printed-on-paper output). The way this works is simplicity itself; it goes

    PRINT "(YOUR MESSAGE HERE)"

You just type in PRINT, and then enclose the message to be printed in quotation marks. When you hit RETURN, the computer puts out your message. In a burst of unappreciated flattery towards an inanimate object, give this a try:

PRINT "I LOVE MY COMPUTER"

and your faithful computer should echo your sentiment.

Already it's time to address the gruesome subject of fallibility. Look around on your keyboard for an "eraser" key such as DEL, BACK-SPACE, or RUBOUT. This will let you erase lines backwards as you go. Try typing in

PRINT "I LXVE MY CXMPX"

and then gobble it all up back to the letter *I* using whatever key you have as an eraser (I'll say DEL for consistency). Note that if you RETURN (RET for short) a fragment like PRIN, the computer will come back with ? SYNTAX ERROR or a similar remark. Some computers have a provision for entering all BASIC key words like PRINT with a single keystroke. If this is the case, DEL will eat the whole word PRINT in one chomp.

Try this longer remark:

PRINT "I LOVE MY COMPUTER AND AM OVERJOYED WITH
ITS POWER"

From now on you will have to remember to hit RETURN after each statement line and immediate commands like RUN. It will start to drive you crazy if this book lists RET or ENTER after each line. You will learn two things from this. First, your computer will adjust any message to its display size. If you have a computer with a small display length, look up some comments for your machine in the appendix of this book. On many small computers, the line above spills over into two lines. Second, it is just nicer to have short lines to type than long lines. The programs we will be using have simple enough output that not much line-typing is needed.

EXERCISE 3
The Uses of "Print," Continued

It is also possible to do a little arithmetic with the PRINT statement, and in fact this amounts to using the computer as a pocket calculator. Just to make things challenging, try this sample:

    PRINT 2+2

and look for the answer at the top of the screen. To illustrate a few points, try the following as well:

    PRINT 67−33
    PRINT 5*9
    PRINT 8/9
    PRINT 2↑3
    PRINT 5.33↑6.4

The first few small points to note are that the "*" symbol means "times" and the "↑" means "to the power of." On some keyboards a little upside down "∨" is used for this, like so "∧," and in a few cases there is a special double asterisk: "**." Just check your manual. (For a little review, 2↑3 means 2 * 2 * 2, 4↑5 means 4 * 4 * 4 * 4 * 4, 10↑2 means 10 * 10 = 100, etc.)

Another point is that computers typically give their numerical results as eight or nine digits, rounded off automatically; consider the case of 8 / 9, which is really 0.888888888 . . . (with eights going on forever) but must be presented in finite form on the computer. This will present a choice in programs about money—one can do some work on output and force the results to show two decimal places, giving answers like PAYMENT = $129.45, or one can write simpler programs that leave the result as PAYMENT = $129.44876 and round off the result when it is copied from the screen to paper.

The last point in connection with these examples is that the computer will enable you to explore the implications of your money decisions in a much more concrete way than has been possible in the past. Can you figure out $(1.0 + 9 / 1200)↑360$ in your head? This sort of computation is easy to get wrong even on a calculator, which typically only lets you see one number at a time, rather than a whole expression. Yet this expression has a lot to do with your life if you are sitting on a thirty-year mortgage. With just a little practice in the simple programs in this book, you will begin to feel comfortable with all types of financial calculation.

Running Instead of Walking

The PRINT statements above have all been executed in immediate mode, i.e., executed (with RET) right after they were entered. When statements are preceded by a *line number*, they will typically be executed upon entering a RUN instruction. Try this sequence:

```
10 PRINT "HELLO, FRED"
RUN
```

When the RUN instruction is entered, the computer looks up all the numbered statements, in this case only one of them, and begins executing them in order. A little variety can be introduced into this situation with the GOTO instruction, which, just as the name implies, tells the computer to go to a numbered line. Now call this little program back onto the screen with the command LIST. This convenient command will be used extensively to review and modify programs. If you now press in

```
20 GOTO 10
```

you will see this added to the earlier statement. This little program will execute statement 10, thus printing the line, and then execute statement 20, which just tells it to go back to 10 and print the same line again. The computer thus fills the screen with its greeting. Some of these machines will stop automatically when the screen is filled, but more typically they will run on forever, with the last message blinking as an intimation of infinity. In that case, you need to find a key for STOP or BREAK or another means of interrupting the program. Once more, there are several common ways of doing this and you will have to consult your manual.

EXERCISE 5
First Inklings of Reality

It is time to say good-bye to Fred. You can get rid of this little program with the instruction NEW (or in some cases CLEAR). You will always erase whatever program is in the computer by using NEW, so be careful with it! You should see the cursor come up and also a remark such as READY or OK, indicating that your tireless computer is ready for a new challenge.

Now we will see about getting some numbers into the computer, since getting numbers in and out of the computer is basically the topic of this book. Try this small program:

```
10 INPUT A
20 PRINT A
RUN
```

What happens? When this program is RUN, the typical computer puts out a question mark to indicate that it is waiting for data. Type in a number and hit RETURN again. The program resumes execution and dutifully prints the number you just entered. Not too dramatic, but this is the start of more useful things.

This type of input is pretty difficult in practice, because on anything longer than a test sample, you are unlikely to remember what the computer wants for input. Call the program up using LIST and add (just type them in and the friendly computer will put everything in the right order)

```
 8 PRINT "A="
20 PRINT "A=";A
```

Now RUN this package; note how the new statement 20 erases the old one automatically. It's no wonder that several manufacturers have gone to the trouble of working out a single-keystroke format for commands—you can probably understand how annoying it is to have a long program "bounce" on a computer because you typed IPNUT somewhere instead of INPUT.

When this program is run it should make two points clear: first, it is nice to have the computer ask for numbers by name and label them when they come back out; second, when you use a semicolon in a PRINT statement, the results are printed right next to each other on the same line (try a comma instead of a semicolon and see what difference it makes).

EXERCISE 6
Making Life Easier

The substitution of a comma for a semicolon can usually be made very easily using your computer's editing capabilities. Suppose we start with the program from the previous exercise:

```
8 PRINT "A="
10 INPUT A
20 PRINT "A=";A
```

It is of course possible to change the semicolon in line 20 to a comma by typing in a new line 20; that's what had to be done in the previous exercise, and for short lines it is not too troublesome. But most computers have a provision for cruising around in the text of your program using the cursor (look for keys on your keyboard with little direction arrows on them). Typically, all you have to do is move the cursor to the place where you want to make a change and just type in the new character over the original one. Some computers come with rather fancy editing functions, but these differ so widely from one machine to the next it will have to be the manufacturer's job to explain them.

Although this book is about the rather grim business of money, and in particular about the even grimmer business of saving yourself from living your whole life as an interest slave, there is no denying that cruising around a program text with the little arrows and editing things with replacement and DEL is often lots of fun. Programs can be as much fun as games!

EXERCISE 7
Reality Revisited

This next piece of work will bring us perilously close to real programming. We will make up a little program that takes an input and squares it, that is, multiplies it by itself. Here is the beginning of such a program:

```
10 PRINT "ENTER A NUMBER"
20 INPUT X
30 PRINT "YOUR NUMBER="; X
40 PRINT "ITS SQUARE IS "; X*X
```

When you run this program, you will probably find that it is indeed a good idea to load programs with reminders about what is going on. There is a special command REM (for "reminder") in BASIC just for this purpose, and we could insert a line

```
5 REM THIS PROGRAM SQUARES NUMBERS
```

which would always print out in the program listing but be ignored by the computer. This book will take a different approach; the programs are meant to fit, typically, in 1K RAM or less, and under these slightly crowded circumstances valuable program line space will be used for messages that actually appear on the screen when the programs are run. This is just a matter of programming style, and the style here will be predicated on the realistic assumption that prompting is always helpful. You may consider the whole book to be a giant REM.

In this last example, we are still doing our arithmetic in PRINT statements, but it is now time to get sophisticated. The main arithmetic statement in BASIC is LET, which makes assignments. That is,

```
LET A=4
```

assigns the value 4 to the variable or symbol A, so that if you now were to tell the computer to PRINT A, it would put a 4 up on the screen. The next step up from this simple assignment is the use of LET in arithmetic. If we have already said

    LET A=4

then the statement

    LET B=2*A

is going to assign the value 8 to B. These LET statements
can be made very complicated, although in this book lines
will be kept short, deliberately, so that they will be easy
to type in correctly. If you have followed all the information presented up to this point, perhaps it is time to give
you the good news that all the programs in this book are
going to be of considerable value to you even if you don't
know personally that 2*4=8. The computer knows, and
that's enough.

  The LET statement can be introduced into our current
program by adding the line

    35 LET Z=X*X

and changing line 40 to

    40 PRINT "ITS SQUARE IS"; Z

You may run this a few times to convince yourself that
this program is functionally the same as the earlier one.
A version in which the computation line was

    35 LET Z=X↑2

would be the same.

Decisions

The computer can do more than just chug through its
program line numbers in sequence, because it has a variety
of decision functions. This book is only going to need a
handful of decision programs, and to write them it is only
going to need one very simple statement structure: IF . . .
THEN GOTO. It is possible to tack a few statements onto
the "squares" program now in the computer to make it
more convenient to use. Try adding these lines to "squares"
above (call it up with LIST to get a good look at it):

```
50 PRINT "AGAIN? YES=1,NO=0"
60 INPUT D
70 IF D=1 THEN GOTO 10
80 STOP
```

If you look at this little piece of program, it's not too hard to figure out what it's telling the computer to do. The computer tells whoever is running the program that it expects an input; if the input is the number 1, the computer goes back to the top, at line 10, and cooks up another square. Although we have said NO=0, in fact *any* other input will stop the computer, because the next line only checks to see if the input D (for decision) is the number 1 or not. If you respond to the prompt with 0, the computer will stop, but it will also stop if you feed it a dollar sign or asterisk or the message "howdy." Give it a few tries and you will discover what sort of error messages your version of BASIC provides; some versions will forgive you all day and keep asking for inputs, and some will clank out a few harsh words.

When you run this program, you will see that even very tiny programs can begin to give the illusion that you are "talking" to the computer. Only this simple type of decision will be needed to make some of the programs in this book seem fairly friendly and interactive.

EXERCISE 9
Over and Over Again

There is actually only one more programming structure with which you should be familiar before applying the programs in this book (you may note by comparing this chapter to the computer manual that all the parts about graphics and plotting and mathematical functions have been left out; these can be absolutely fascinating but they have nothing to do with money and thus, crassly, are omitted here). This structure is the one that directs the computer to perform some action repetitively. After all, to a certain extent, what makes computers valuable is their willingness to crank through the same boring calculations over again. If you still have the old program in the computer, enter NEW to clear it and try this fragment:

```
10 FOR N=1 TO 10
20 PRINT N
30 NEXT N
```

Run it and see what happens. Although most of the microcomputers used these days can work this out in a millisecond or so, some of them have such slow display management that the computer appears to be counting like a four-year-old. Others fill the screen so fast it looks like it's exploding. *Anything* you have bought will be plenty fast enough for the calculations we will be doing.

A variation on this program may be obtained by replacing this line 20 with another one:

```
20 PRINT "LET'S DO THIS TEN TIMES"
```

What happened to "N" in this example? It is simply used as a counter, and since we don't ask the computer to do anything with it, it doesn't show up in the output. Try sticking this back in the program:

```
15 PRINT N
```

and running the program again (among other things, this shows how many times that statement was printed). As a further slight variant, erase statement 20 by just typing 20 and RETURN, and insert this:

```
15 PRINT N,N*N
```

and when the program is run it prints a nice little table of squares.

Believe it or not, with this rather modest background you are now ready to set forth into the world of financial programming. While it may not be sporting to tell you this so far in advance, what you will find is that most calculations in this area can be done very easily, thanks to the computer. Rather fancy operations, such as finding out how much of your payment has gone for interest after nineteen months of a 48-month consumer loan, will turn out to be quick work in a short program. The idea here is that perhaps you will want to learn a little more about programming if programming has ever done you any good, e.g., saved you some money. Onward!

Financial BASIC:
A Very Short Course

Most of the calculations undertaken in this book will involve straightforward use of standard formulas that have been known in financial practice for centuries. These calculations can be done with specialized "business" calculators on which the little keys are labeled "PMT," "FV," "I," and so forth. We will present a review of these calculations, but we will also note that there are impressive advantages to doing this kind of work on a computer. These advantages are:

- The computer can be programmed to ask for needed information in a readily recognized way. It will ask for inputs as words, such as "TOTAL LOAN AMOUNT," instead of expecting you to know which lump of money is "FV" in each kind of problem.
- The computer is flexible. For example, if you have a financial calculator, what do you think you should do to calculate the real return on savings at 9% when the inflation rate is 11%? (Hint: you can't do it first at 9 and then at 11 and divide the answers.) Yet this situation is no problem at all to handle in a BASIC program, and once more, all you have to understand is the meaning of the problem, not the equations.
- The computer can present different cases for easy comparison on the screen at the same time. The single-number display on even expensive business calculators is truly unhelpful in this regard.

This chapter will cover a few basic situations, showing how financial formulas are derived. Later in the book, some formulas will appear in programs without much explanation, on the assumption that the reader is probably more immediately concerned about money than mathematics. What will rapidly become clear in all these situations is that only a few basic routines are needed to cover all types of finance; banks have definitely figured out how they like to do business.

The Starting Point: Compound Interest

Simple interest is beneath the dignity of your computer since it represents a single multiplication performed only once. If you borrow $2,000 at 8% simple interest for one year, at the end of the year you owe the original $2,000 plus $160, which is 8% of $2,000 (0.08*2000). If you can pardon such a horrid pun, this situation is not very interesting. Thus compound interest was born.

The standard modification of the situation involving the $2,000 might go like so: instead of simple interest, the 8% will be taken as nominal annual 8%, compounded monthly. This means that the 8% is divided into twelve little chunks, as

8% = 0.08 annual = 0.08/12 = 0.0066667 monthly

In the simple-interest case, the total amount owed at the end of the loan period was

$2,000 * (1 + 0.08) = $2,000 + $160 = $2,160

In the compound-interest case, the same formula is used, but it is used monthly, and in each succeeding month the interest term will apply to the original $2,000 and the smaller interest term also. The schedule goes this way:

First month: total = $2,000 * (1 + .0066667) = $2,013.33
Second month: total = $2,013.33 * (1 + .0066667) = $2,026.76
Third month: total = $2,026.76 * (1 + .0066667) = $2,040.27

and so on, for twelve months.

This is clearly a case for a program. We will stick

to the numbers at hand for the moment to be specific, and then work up a general example.

```
10 LET AMT=2000
20 LET INT=0.08/12
30 LET Z=(1+INT)
40 FOR K=1 TO 12
50 LET AMT=AMT*Z
60 NEXT K
70 PRINT "TOTAL OWED=$";AMT
```

This should show a total owed of $2,165.999, which your lender will undoubtedly be willing to round off to $2,166. It is always possible to round off these dollar totals on the computer, but at the cost of putting in three or four lines of fussy output typing; thus we are going to round off by hand (really, it will be less work). The main point here is that the interest works out to be more than it was in the simple-interest example because of the monthly compounding. In this case the difference is only $6; for longer time periods and higher interest rates the effect of compounding is much more impressive.

The program above gives as its answer the quantity AMT, which was the original AMT multiplied by Z twelve times. The compact notation for this quantity on the computer would just be the expression AMT*(Z↑12), of AMT times the quantity Z to the power 12. Let's stick in this patch at the end of the existing program:

```
 80 STOP
 90 LET AMT=2000*(Z↑12)
100 GOTO 70
```

Run this part of the program by typing in GOTO 90. What happens? The same answer appears, since the two statements are equivalent. Actually, some computers may give answers that are different in the last decimal place; this depends on the details of number representation in the computer and its effects on accuracy. Any computer you can buy has more than enough accuracy for the kind of work we will be doing.

The calculation above turns out to be this formula from the financial handbooks:

$$FV = PV * (1 + I){\uparrow}N$$

or as it actually appears in those works:

$$FV = PV \times (1 + i)^n$$

This expression contains four of the five quantities that comprise the whole universe of finance (the other one is PMT, or payment, and will appear shortly). Here is a short introduction to these ubiquitous variables:

FV Future value of an amount of money. If you borrowed the money, the future value is the $2,166 that you have to pay. If you had deposited the $2,000 in a bank for 8% compounded monthly, the future value, $2,166, is what your deposit will be worth.

PV Present value of an amount of money. That's the $2,000 in the example above. In a mortgage calculation, PV is the amount you are trying to get from the bank (FV is what you will end up paying over the years).

N Number of time intervals for compounding. It's 12 in this example because we compounded monthly for a year. Banks can get very precise about this, compounding daily and taking leap years into account.

I Interest rate, specifically the rate per compounding period. That's why 8%/12 is used instead of 8% in this monthly example.

The Next Step: Payments Plus Interest

Regular payments introduce one more level of complication into these calculations, but it really isn't too difficult. Suppose you had the $2,000 above and were putting it in a bank to earn the 8% interest. We will change the interest rules and your finances to go like this: every year you will take $2,000 on December 31 and put it in the

bank, and the bank will pay 8% per year, but not compounded monthly. This routine will go on for twenty years.
How much money will you have at the end of the twenty
years? Let's run up the beginning of this computation by
hand to see how a program might work:

First year: $2,000 (deposited last day of year;
          no interest)
Next year: $2,000 * (1 + 0.08) + $2,000
Next year: $2,000 * (1 + 0.08) * (1 + 0.08) + $2,000
          * (1 + 0.08) + $2,000

In the first year there is just the payment itself; in
the next year there is that year's payment, plus last year's
with its interest. By the third year the original deposit
has been sitting around for two interest periods, last year's
has picked up one round of interest, and there is of course
the current year's deposit. This is something of a nuisance
as a handwork problem. Fortunately, there are two forms
of possible salvation: first, this is a simple computer situation, and second, there is a convenient algebraic formula
that takes into account these repeated interest multiplica-
tions.

The program is fairly tidy and just steps through the
sequence shown. Try typing this in:

```
10 LET AMT=2000
20 LET Z=(1+0.08)
30 LET SUM=AMT
40 FOR K=1 TO 19
50 LET AMT=AMT*Z
60 LET SUM=SUM+AMT
70 NEXT K
80 PRINT "TOTAL=$";SUM
```

If you are interested in programming, you should step
this through a few cycles and see that it really does what
it should (if you're not interested in programming, you
can skip this whole chapter anyway with no adverse consequences).

Running the program should give you the result $91,523.929 (just make that 93¢ there, thanks). You may have noticed, by the way, the overwhelming resemblance between the scheme outlined here and the basic savings-and-loan IRA (individual retirement account).

The algebraic formula for this same situation is:

$$FV = PMT * ((1 + I){\uparrow}N - 1) / I$$

where for this example PMT is the $2,000, N is 20, and I is 0.08, meaning 8%. You can append this formula to the program as

```
90 LET SUM=2000*((Z↑20)−1)/0.08
100 PRINT SUM
```

and run it by typing in GOTO 90. Watch to see if you get exactly the same answer (you probably will).

There will be some occasions on which it is possible to do interesting things with a FOR . . . NEXT loop, and then other occasions on which it will be better to use the algebraic method to condense the computation to a single line. Usually, in this book, a choice of calculation will be made on the basis of ease of program entry rather than mathematical elegance.

The Last Word: Regular Payments

The two expressions above can be combined to give one line that tells what PMT, your payments, will be, in terms of PV, the amount of money you are trying to borrow. It's really quite simple as an algebra problem; just equate the two different forms above for FV and you are left with an equation that contains PMT on one side, and PV, N, and I on the other. What emerges is this:

$$PMT = PV * I / (1 - (1 + I){\uparrow}(-N))$$

which may be incorporated into a small program to run the now-famous problem of the $2,000 as a monthly-payment example. The program is:

```
10 PRINT "INPUT AMT, N, I"
20 INPUT PV
30 INPUT N
40 INPUT I
50 LET PMT=PV*I/(1−(1+I)↑(−N))
60 PRINT "PMT=$";PMT
```

This is a stripped-down version of nicer programs that won't require you to know much about how they work. In this case, you have to run our example by responding to the INPUT prompt with

2000 (RET)
12 (RET)
0.08/12 (RET)

because the appropriate interest rate is the monthly interest (8%) divided by the number of compounding terms (12). You should be rewarded for your labors by the answer

PMT=$173.97685

and you can also enter the statement PRINT PMT*12 to find that over the year the payments have totaled $2,087.7223. This is less than the total in the wait-to-the-end-of-the-year mode of payment because not all of the money is out at interest for the whole year.

The Word after the Last Word

Most of the programs in the next section of the book are either variations or particularizations of the easy BASIC programs just presented. The idea here is that if you are interested in some topic, for example, car leasing, you turn to the section on cars, find the leasing program, type it in, and save it on cassette tape (a few hints are to be offered forthwith). Unless you are exceptionally curious, rich, or greedy, you won't need very many programs from the whole collection all at once; but you will find the programs are short enough to be entered in just two to five minutes or so, and make a reasonably informative short session at the computer.

First hint   Look through the book and find a program on a topic you find interesting. Type it in and then run it. In the course of putting in a real program of reasonable length (fifteen lines or so), you will develop a lot of motivation to find out about editing on your computer. Once you get used to the editing facilities available, everything you have to do in this book will become practically trivial.

Second hint   Learn how to save your programs on tape (if you have a disk drive instead, good for you—all the programs in the whole book will fit in about 20K of disk space). You may find that at any given time you are only interested in one type of calculation, e.g., credit cards; in that case, just put the credit card programs on tape and *label the tape*! This will all get confusing in a hurry if you don't keep things neatly labeled. If you read through chapters of interest first, you will see that you can save yourself considerable typing—many of the programs build on earlier ones, and you can load the core programs from tape, add a few lines, and save the new program under a new name.

None of this will be difficult, and unless you are a professional diamond smuggler, a great deal of it will be useful. On that cheerful note, look ahead and find something interesting!

3
Credit Cards

Credit cards, for better or worse, have become a standard method for buying small or medium-priced consumer items in the United States. This is a source of astonishment to the citizens of other nations; people from Taiwan and Japan are frequently amazed at the prevalence of credit-card use here. (On the other hand, Americans are amazed to hear of businessmen in those countries safely carrying around their payrolls in cash from the bank to the office.) It is not unusual to be offered department-store credit cards over the phone, or gasoline-company credit cards through the mail. A few months ago the author was invited to accept a "prestige" credit card, apparently for no other reason than that he subscribed to a magazine (the name was identically misspelled on both the subscription and the card offer). At this level of encouragement, there's not much way of escaping this phenomenon.

Curiously, as credit cards run rampant, the firms that used to handle consumer credit in installment plans are falling all over themselves in their haste to replace such plans with credit cards. When this is done, it is accompanied by great assurances that the two forms of credit are really equivalent. In the older and more traditional format, you would go to a department store, buy a refrigerator, and be signed up for a three-year installment-payment routine. The current way this would typically be done would be simply to put the refrigerator on a charge card. The advantages for the store in the new scheme are twofold. First, if you read the fine print, with a credit card the store can change the interest rate on you at any time.

This became a big item with the stores, as you may expect, when interest and inflation rates began to blow up simultaneously in the late 1970s. Second, the bookkeeping on cards is much simpler; there is no complicated arithmetic to do if you decide to pay the loan back early, and the store can allow you to run up your tab even further without rewriting your paperwork.

The credit-card system referred to here will be the standard form of bank card, i.e., Mastercard and VISA, which in a remarkable coincidence have virtually the same terms, no matter which bank offers them. Another remarkable coincidence is that, although interest rates on other forms of lending have dropped from their historic high points in the earlier 1980s, the banks, being true gentlemen, are declining the opportunity to compete with each other on the basis of interest rates (there are lots of attractive TV commercials out there, however).

Programming with Plastic Money

Here is a sampling of programs of general interest to those laboring under the sometimes slippery burden of credit card debt. Most of these programs are developed first in simplest form and then "decorated" or otherwise slightly improved. Just pick the version that most closely suits your interests:

Program 3A: $500 or Less on a Credit Card
This program computes the eventual cost of a $500 item when it is bought on a typical bank credit card and paid back at a minimum monthly rate.

Program 3B: Credit Cards—Over $500
Interestingly enough, this does not turn out to be just like the previous example. Large sums create a different situation.

Program 3C: Credit Cards with Inflation
For given inflation rates and your tax bracket, the results of A and B are recomputed in constant dollars.

Program 3D: Installment Interest Rates
This program compares the two ways of financing consumer purchases. It contains the calculation for early payment on installment plans.

Program 3E: Refinance Cost
One way to get rid of credit card debt is to refinance it into a long-term low-interest loan such as a home loan. This program evaluates the consequences of refinancing.

Five Hundred Dollars
on Its Way through the System

The seemingly arbitrary cut-off at $500 is imposed by bank rules, which operate a little differently for smaller amounts like this. On the back of the typical bank-card monthly-payment form it clearly states, in fairly tiny print:

If your new balance is	Your minimum periodic payment is
Less than $20	The amount of your new balance
$20 to $500	$20 plus any amount of previous minimum payment past due

This is clear enough; the bank just wants $20 per month until you have a last payment of less than $20 (of course, at this point you may be so pleased with yourself that you go out and celebrate on the card, but that issue is moral rather than computational). On the front of the payment form is the monthly interest rate, which for many cards is running about 1.67%. This gives the bank an annual return of 20% or so on credit-card debt, which explains why banks will frequently raise their credit line for you unless you have absolutely been disgracing yourself. Consult one of your forms right now and find out the actual monthly interest in your own case, since it may differ slightly from the figure above (the current range seems to be about 1.55% to 1.8%); you will need this number for the program.

For a first pass, to see how the program is constructed,

consider the first month with your $500. The bank will ask for $20, but 500*(0.0167) of this, or $8.35, is interest, so $11.65 is actually contributed toward reducing your debt. The next month the interest will be applied to the remaining balance, which is $488.35, and once more the $20 payment for the month will be nearly half interest. Thus we need to make a loop that does this:

a. figure interest part of payment
b. take out $20 from total but add back interest
c. keep cycling through (a) and (b) until the total is less than $20

Here is a beginning version of such a program:

PROGRAM 3A
$500 or Less on a Credit Card

```
  5 LET Z=0.0167
 10 PRINT "ENTER AMT"
 20 INPUT T
 30 PRINT "AMT=$";T
 40 LET PT=0
 50 FOR K=1 TO 100
 60 LET I=Z*T
 70 LET T=T−20+I
 80 LET PT=PT+20
 90 IF T<=20 THEN GOTO 120
100 NEXT K
120 LET PT=PT+T
130 PRINT "PMT TOTAL=$";PT
```

COMMENTS
- PT in this program is the counter that is totaling up payments. Every time the program goes through the loop, it rings up another $20 and adds it to the total.
- Line 5 puts in the interest rate (use the one the bank is actually charging you, if yours is different from 1.67%). This value is put in the program this way for two reasons: first, it makes it easy to change, since a call to EDIT starts

at this line; second, it is easier to make sure this important number is correctly typed in when it is on its own line, rather than entered as part of a formula.
- The decision in line 90 has been presented this way to show correspondence with the line of reasoning presented. RUN a few sample calculations and then replace it with

    90 IF T<=19.666 THEN GOTO 120

before making a copy on tape. This is tricky; if you start the month owing, say, $19.80, the interest makes it more than $20, so it's not quite the last minimum payment. This new line makes the split exactly.

We will try five rounds of sample output to see if this example contains a real take-home lesson (shouldn't say that really—it's an old school expression and you are probably at home anyway). RUN the program for the values $500, $400, $300, $200, $100, and $50. You should be able to construct this table from the results:

Amount	Payment total
$500	$652.44
$400	$490.70
$300	$348.11
$200	$220.64
$100	$105.24
$ 50	$ 51.35

To dramatize the point this table intends to make, here is a plot that shows the amount of the payments total divided by the original amount, charted against the original amount.

The lesson here is that the amount of money you eventually pay out in interest starts to climb pretty rapidly for larger amounts. The minimum monthly payment is designed to be a delicate balance between the bank's need to cover the costs of its paperwork and its burning desire to lend people as much money as possible at 20% annual

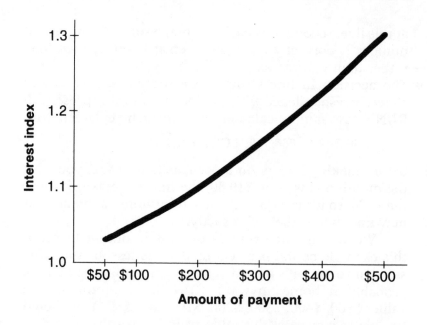

interest. For your own amusement, you might want to see what would happen if the minimum payment for $500 charged on this type of card were $10 per month instead; for those of you who don't feel like making the program modification, the answer is $1,081, which works out to nine years of payments! A sinister variation of this is to try a minimum payment of $8; since this is less than the first interest payment, the computer never comes back (the loop size on K would have to be infinite) and the bill never gets paid off. This fascinating principle is of course fabled in song and story as the routine at the "company store" in mining towns earlier in this century. All the store has to do is advance amounts of credit smaller than the interest payments!

If the conclusion that you are drawing from all this is that you should try to pay a little more than the minimum payment each time, you can ponder this information as well: if you decide to accelerate your payments on the $500 to $35 per month, the total of payments will be about $576 instead of $652. This plot thickens further in the next program.

$2,000 and Up:
Financing the Lost Weekend in Acapulco

Actually, if your problem is that stated in this section head, congratulations. Despite the efforts of certain persons in government to portray average citizens as wanton spendthrifts who need a dose of strong medicine (and of course, this advice is never directed against people who are actually rich), it happens that recent surveys suggest that consumer debt is rising because people are no longer able to afford car repairs, medical and dental expenses, children's clothes, and so forth, and have for the last few years taken to charging these expenses. Those frivolous little rascals—some stiff credit terms will soon show them the error of their heedless ways! (Please excuse the very occasional outburst of this type; evaluating money problems in a society where some people can get a 9% loan for a Mercedes while other people have to charge baby medicine at 22% has sometimes been a rather curious experience. If you're writing about banking, you're writing about politics, whether you like it or not.)

A program to run up totals in this case raises a choice. The computation changes at $500, because on amounts over this, the minimum payment per month is supposed to be 4% of the outstanding balance. Now a straightforward way to do this would have these elements:

a. section to start values for PT and amount charged
b. FOR . . . NEXT loop, which runs until total is below $500, at which point control jumps down to another loop
c. the other loop, which handles cases under $500 and looks just like Program 3A above

This will work as a program, but there are two features of it that aren't as nice as they could be. First, if we were to do the program this way, you would find yourself typing in a lot of very similar lines twice. That is never much fun, and certainly fails to amuse the beginning programmer. Second, it is not satisfying as a solution to a programming problem, because the only real difference between this case and 3A is that now the program must figure out a payment size based on the balance. It should be possible to stick in a little patch about payment-size decision and save most of the effort of rewriting the program. Also, the new program will fit in very little memory in the computer.

So call up Program 3A from cassette tape or memory and try this. If you have just jumped into the book at this point, don't worry; a complete listing of the program is about to follow anyway. Change lines 70 and 80 to these:

```
70 LET T=T—PM+I
80 LET PT=PT+PM
```

Add these lines:

```
62 IF T<=500 THEN GOTO 68
64 LET PM=T*0.04
66 GOTO 70
68 LET PM=20
```

There's nothing especially mysterious about this; it just makes the payment decision at each step and proceeds on its way. This is very slightly wasteful of the computer's time (note that we keep reassigning PM to 20 over and over again) and the program takes a few seconds to run. But sometimes it's fun to watch the computer take a while . . . the suspense is dramatic.

Let's get the program listing out and then look at a few cases.

PROGRAM 3B

Credit Cards—Over $500

```
 5 LET Z=0.0167
10 PRINT "ENTER AMT"
20 INPUT T
30 PRINT "AMT=$";T
40 LET PT=0
50 FOR K=1 TO 100
60 LET I=Z*T
```

```
62 IF T<=500 THEN GOTO 68
64 LET PM=T*0.04
66 GOTO 70
78 LET PM=20
70 LET T=T−PM+I
80 LET PT=PT+PM
90 IF T<=19.666 THEN GOTO 120
100 NEXT K
120 LET PT=PT+T
130 PRINT "PMT TOTAL=$";PT
```

First, it is worthwhile to run this program with the value $500 for the input amount, just to check that it is still all right. If everything has been typed in properly, you should get the same answer you got in the first case, $652.44 (remember, we're doing our own rounding off). You will probably note that this program runs a little slower than the earlier version.

Next, try a few cases to see the effect of trying larger amounts. Just to keep track of things, toss in the line

```
140 PRINT "NO. OF PMTS=";K
```

This will show us how long the payback period lasts. For the cases $1000, $1500, and $2000, your program should yield the data in this table:

Amount	Payment total	Number of payments
$1,000	$1,510.93	62
$1,500	$2,369.26	79
$2,000	$3,227.59	91

What a curious business this is! The way this is shaping up, it looks like for larger debts the total payment is going to be about half again what you charged. To confirm this, if you have the patience, change the index in the FOR loop so that it can run up to 300, and run the program for a starting debt of $10,000. What seems like a lifetime later (actually about a minute), the computer comes back with $16,961 as the payments total after 159 months of payments! What is going on here?

Well, what's happening is pretty simple. On amounts larger than $500, the bank sets the payments at 4% of the total and charges 1.67% interest per pass. Your first $400 payment on the $10,000 is $233 worth of payment on the principal and $167 worth of payment in interest. Thus the "interest factor" will be

$$(400 / 233) = 1.717$$

and in a long enough term, this factor tells you what you will ultimately pay on the original debt. Note that this factor gives a pretty good approximation even for $1,000— it suggests you would pay $1,717 in the long run, whereas you actually pay $1,510 because you pay it off more rapidly (more rapidly than forever, at any rate). What you might want to consider while shopping, if you have a credit-card balance over $1000, is that anything you see for $100 will eventually cost you $160 or so if you charge it and don't pay it back that month. Informative, no?

Inflation and Taxes Come to Your Rescue?

Not quite, but if you have borrowed money in an inflationary period, inflation will be gradually reducing the real-dollar value of your payments. Furthermore, the interest on your payments will be tax-deductible. With a few approximations, it is possible to work out the constant-dollar expense of a credit-card purchase. The tax part will be easy enough, and to consider the effect of inflation it is only necessary to include a depreciation term on PT in the earlier programs. Call up your tape copy of Program 3B and enter these four lines:

```
  7 LET F=0.995
 75 LET PR=PM*F↑(K−1)
 80 LET PT=PT+PR
120 LET PT=PT+T*F↑(K−1)
```

This should give you the following program, which we proudly display as:

PROGRAM 3C
Credit Cards with Inflation

```
 5 LET Z=0.0167
 7 LET F=0.995
10 PRINT "ENTER AMT"
20 INPUT T
30 PRINT "AMT=$";T
40 LET PT=0
50 FOR K=1 TO 100
60 LET I=Z*T
62 IF T<=500 THEN GOTO 68
64 LET PM=T*0.04
66 GOTO 70
68 LET PM=20
70 LET T=T−PM+I
75 LET PR=PM*F↑(K−1)
80 LET PT=PT+PR
90 IF T<=19.666 THEN GOTO 120
100 NEXT K
120 LET PT=PT+T*F↑(K−1)
130 PRINT "PMT TOTAL=$";PT
```

This program really takes a long time, but the output when it arrives is fairly interesting; the computing interval affords ample opportunity for meditation on mankind's hopes and fears. Please observe what has been done here. There is an inflation flag set in line 7. The value $F=0.995$ as depreciation corresponds to an inflation rate of 0.5% per month, or a little more than 6% per year when suitably compounded. (F's value is determined by the formula "1−interest due," which in this case is .5%, or .005. Likewise, $F=0.99$ would mean 1% inflation per month, and so forth.) A set of test cases with the rate set to $F=0.995$ or an annual rate of about 6.2% yields this table:

Amount	Total payments	"Real" total (adjusted)
$400	$491	$464
$1,000	$1,511	$1,328
$2,000	$3,228	$2,763

Consider for a moment the case of the $1,000. If you are in the 20% tax bracket, the fact of the $511 total interest being deductible means that the real effective cost to you is 80% of $511, which is $409, and you are spared about $102 in expense. (Remember, deductible doesn't really work out to mean it's free, it just represents an odd sort of discount.) But the expense for interest in real dollars turned out to be only $328, of which you have saved yourself $109. The total "service charge" on the whole package in constant dollars is about half what it appears to be in nominal dollars before taxes.

Whether this business about constant dollars vs. nominal dollars will do you any good personally depends on whether you can expect cost-of-living raises. If so, everything is great, and your payments will get easier as time goes on; if not, you are stuck with the payments on your same old salary with the same dollars you were getting when the payments began. This is a serious point to consider, since most occupations are showing a range of indices against inflation, from about 5% ahead to 10% behind.

If you run this program with F = 0.9833, you will have picked an inflation rate that matches the credit-card interest rate, and thus will get back the same value (plus or minus a few bucks for slight imprecision in the inflation time interval in the program) as payment total that you plug in for amount borrowed. In fact, you would come out ahead, since all your interest payments were deductible. But the banks know that 20% inflation per year is not immediately likely, for five continuous years at least, and have hedged themselves against this rather ghastly prospect anyway by allowing themselves to raise their rates if necessary. Ultimately, what emerges from this exercise is that in practice your real effective rate on credit-card borrowing, after taxes and allowing for moderate inflation, will be between 60% and 85% of the apparent rate stated on the monthly bill. This may not be the best news in the world, but it will have to do until you get lucky.

Credit Cards vs. Installment Plans

The traditional way of financing consumer purchases, the most common way before credit cards took over most of the business, was the installment plan. This method is still used when the sums of money are large; for example, it is pretty much the way car financing is done at the car companies' financial service groups. The computation of payment is delightfully simple, and goes like this:

a. take the amount financed, say $4,000;
b. take the "annual rate," say 12%, and multiply it by the number of years, which we will take to be four in this example;
c. then the add-on interest, as it is called, is 12%∗4 = 0.48 times the amount financed; in this case, 0.48∗$4,000 = $1,920;
d. the four-year-loan period is 48 months, and the total amount owed is now considered to be $4,000 + $1,920 = $5,920, so the monthly payments are going to be $5,920/48 = $123.33.

There is a subtle point about interest here, one that the lenders now cheerfully disclose, being forced to these days by Federal Regulation Z. The "annual rate" in this package is being charged as if you owed the whole $4,000 for the whole four years; this means that the real rate, which corresponds to the "I" used in most of the programs in this book, is actually much higher. This little program is a version of the way the effective rate, called the "APR" on the paperwork (for "annual percentage rate"), is calculated.

PROGRAM 3D
Installment Interest Rate

```
10 PRINT "ENTER PMT, AMT"
20 INPUT P
30 INPUT A
40 PRINT "YRS=?"
50 INPUT NY
55 LET N=NY*12
60 FOR K=1 TO 30
70 LET IX=K/1200
80 LET PX=A*IX/(1−(1+IX)↑(−N))
90 IF P<=PX THEN GOTO 120
100 NEXT K
105 PRINT "APR OVER 30"
110 GOTO 130
120 PRINT "APR BETWEEN ";K−1;"AND ";K
130 STOP
```

Let's RUN this example with the numbers above, entering 123.33 for the payments, 4000 for the amount (remember an ENTER after each number), and 4 for the number of years. After a little wait while the computer runs through its numbers, you should see the message:

```
APR BETWEEN 20 AND 21
```

(Hint: you can speed this up by using the line

```
60 FOR K=10 TO 30
```

instead; not much chance you're going to see an APR lower than 10% anytime soon!)

What all this means is that the lender can announce "12% FINANCING" in huge banners all over the place, but eventually must put into the fine print somewhere that the APR is a little more than 20%. Other than this distinction, there is no difference between the add-on-interest scheme and a fixed-term "mortgage-type" loan. The main difference between both of these and credit cards as a financing plan is that these two have a fixed term in years, no matter what the amount of money, whereas the number of payments on a credit card depends on the size of the starting balance.

With this program and a previous one, it is possible to compare credit cards to installment payments in a table:

	Total payments		Number of payments	
Starting amount	Installment plan	Credit card	Installment plan	Credit card
$2,000	$2,960	$3,228	48	91
$4,000	$5,920	$6,661	48	120

The trend to credit cards from installment payments at department stores was originally provoked by a desire to be able to raise interest rates easily during the course of a loan. Under a credit-card plan, for example, the lender can raise the interest rate while keeping the monthly payments the same; because of the way household money is usually managed, many people find this less objectionable than *lowering* the rate if it raised the payments (through an accelerated payback plan). But it would be a serious nuisance, not worth the few hundred dollars shown, to wait ten years to get a $4,000 loan paid off. In an inflationary period it would not only be a nuisance, it would be pretty bad business. So probably a larger part of the desire of companies to see you with credit cards instead of an installment plan is the expectation that you will run your balance up to somewhere within a few hundred of your credit line and then keep adding purchases as you get the balance partially paid (sound like the holiday season for anyone you know?). When this happens, ordinary department stores get to move into a heavenly realm formerly reserved for national governments, in which they get to collect lots of money just for existing. While the computer is churning away someday running up an APR for you, you could use that bit of time to think about just what kind of borrowing situation you would like to be in.

Refinancing

Part one of a refinancing program is really simple because it doesn't even call for a computer. If you're thinking of tying a lot of smaller credit card debts into a second mortgage or other type of deal at interest rates comparable to credit-card interest (within a few percent), just write

DON'T!

in the middle of a big sheet of white paper and leave it at that. The reasons for such a definite instruction will become clear after a consideration of a more reasonable (though not always worthwhile either) situation, one in which you are refinancing a house anyway. If you are refinancing a house to get a lower rate on the whole house loan, you might consider trying to take out a little more money and getting enough to cover credit-card debts. To evaluate this prospect, you will first need the program that computes credit-card totals adjusted for inflation (Program 3C) and this program:

PROGRAM 3E
Refinance Cost

```
10 PRINT "ENTER AMT"
15 INPUT A
20 PRINT "ENTER INTEREST,INFLATION"
30 INPUT IX
40 INPUT IL
50 PRINT "YRS=?"
60 INPUT N
70 LET I=(IX−IL)/1200
80 LET NM=N*12
90 LET P=A*NM*I/(1−(1+I)↑(−NM))
100 PRINT "PMT TOTAL=$";P
```

Before we run this, let's note a few points. The bank charges you points and a fee for doing a refinance at all (see chapter 5), so the deal better be good from the standpoint of house refinancing in the first place. It's clearly not going to work if you are taking on $2,500 in bank charges to get rid of a $2,000 credit-card loan. Additionally, this program makes a reference to the inflation rate because central to this kind of refinance is the hope that twenty years from now you will be paying off the residue of your old credit-card debt in nearly worthless funny money. The bank knows this, and tries to keep its interest rates accordingly. Thus the attractiveness of this scheme depends on the actual numbers.

Take $4,000 as the example. We will run up the refinance as a thirty-year loan at 12% interest, and try it at inflation rates of 0%, 6%, and 10%. Then for comparison we will call up the inflation-averaged version of the credit-card program.

	Payments in constant dollars	
Inflation rate	Refinance	Credit card
0%	$14,812	$6,661
6%	$ 8,634	$5,580
10%	$ 5,323	$5,094

This table outlines pretty clearly the effect operating in all refinance deals: when you effectively finance the $4,000 as part of a mortgage at 12% for thirty years, the monthly payments become $41, compared to the $160 per month that the credit-card company wants. But in the mortgage case, the result of the smaller payments is that the debt lingers on, piling up interest charges, for decades. As bad as credit-card interest rates are, you would have to find a refinance package at *less than 4% interest* to pay less money over the years, under 0% inflation conditions. Credit cards charge a lot of interest, but they want the money paid off relatively rapidly compared to mortgage lenders.

So, strangely enough, this chapter has a conclusion even for readers who aren't interested in programming: the only way to minimize lifetime interest payments is always to try to pay everything back as quickly as you

can. Easy enough to say, not so easy to do! But it's worth
remembering that every time you are offered easier payments, you are being asked for more total money in the
end, even with fairly brisk inflation and allowing for tax
breaks on interest.

4
Cars

It can hardly have escaped your attention that, for better or worse, things ain't what they used to be in the wonderful world of automobiles. Industry surveys have shown a number of trends that have large and direct bearing on family finances:

- The cost of owning and operating a car has risen faster than the overall inflation rate. Car prices themselves are only partly to blame; gasoline prices and the cost of insurance and repairs have been more responsible.
- The age of the average car on the road in the United States has increased by almost two years from what it was in the late 1960s. This situation, generated by real declines in disposable income and rising car prices, has been especially pronounced at the older end of the scale—many more cars over ten years old are running around out there. This has lots of negative impact on safety and pollution.
- Leasing instead of buying cars, which once was a practice reserved for business, is now a common procedure for ordinary families. Whether this is because leases are a great idea or because no one can afford 20% down payments on $11,000 cars (that's the price of the average General Motors product at the moment) will be considered with the aid of some simple programs.

Various observers have noted that if the auto industry had been doing as well as the computer business during the last twenty years, cars would now cost 29¢ and get twelve thousand miles per gallon of gas. Actually, within the last two or three years, the prices of cars have not been increasing as fast as inflation in general, and gas mileage has been notably improved; this has happened largely because computer-aided design systems have started to find worthwhile material trade-offs and aerodynamic effects, and because computer-managed ignition and fuel-injection systems in the cars themselves have improved in performance and reliability. Now if only the price of hand-dipped chrome exhaust systems and genuine all-lizard-skin interiors would fall, paradise would presumably return to these troubled shores.

Before bursting into tears thinking about the olden days (the author is thinking particularly of a magazine article from 1969 that he carried around for years; it was called "Ten Best Sports Cars Under $2,000"), we may note that the problem that has called for a chapter on cars in this book is not the hardware. The cars themselves are in many cases pretty well stuck together and fun to drive. The problem is that car financing is adding thousands of dollars to the already discouraging sticker prices; financing rates from 15 to 20% over periods of 60 months are now quite common. A $6,000 car ends up costing $10,000 total over a typical five-year financing plan. Under normal usage and $1.50 per gallon gas prices, you can find yourself paying more for interest than for fuel over the life of the car. A little examination of the available ways of purchasing a car is therefore in order. The caution will be advanced, as it is one of the recurring themes of this book, that very often easier terms (meaning lower monthly payments) translate into more expense in the long run; somehow you have to strike a balance between what you can afford right now, and what will ultimately be the best deal.

Plain Vanilla

Straight car purchasing, through banks, credit unions, or the dealers themselves, works on a scheme that can be taken to be either add-on financing or mortgage-like normal time payments. In an add-on scheme, the payments are worked out as

$$\text{payments} = \frac{(\text{car price} + \text{finance charge})}{(\text{number of months})}$$

The finance charge is computed by this formula:

finance charge = years * price * interest rate

where "interest rate" in this case means a number quoted by the lender, which is fictitiously low compared to the real interest rate indicated by "I" in most calculations (the lender must indicate the real rate, called "APR" in this sort of work, somewhere in his advertising, according to law). The interest rate quoted by a bank or credit union is usually the only number offered in the documentation, so it is necessarily the "I" in the calculation. Let's set up a simple payments program and see if something fascinating emerges. Before we do, something fascinating is already clear:

In this scheme you pay interest on the whole loan amount all the time, although the loan balance is progressively paid off. That's why the real rate is so much higher than the "interest rate."

PROGRAM 4A
The Straight Goods

This version will assume as input the total amount to be financed (including tax and license fees), and you will have to take the down payments out of the price yourself. It would be simple to make up a version of the program that would take care of these points, but it isn't convenient in practice; what is usually wanted is a comparison of financing terms for a particular car. The other inputs are the loan terms.

```
10 PRINT "ENTER AMOUNT"
20 INPUT A
30 PRINT "ENTER RATE, MONTHS"
```

```
40 INPUT IX
50 INPUT N
60 PRINT "TOTAL=$";A
70 PRINT IX;" PERCENT, ";N;"MOS"
75 LET I=IX/1200
80 LET P=A∗I/(1−(1+I)↑(−N))
90 PRINT "PAYMENT PER MONTH=$";P
```

Let's check this out on a real-life example taken from a newspaper ad. The vehicle in question is a 1980 Buick Skylark, which the car dealer is willing to finance with no down payment. The total amount to finance is $6,385.74, for 60 months, and the dealer is admirably forthright about announcing the rate as 20.31% (no funny business about 12% financing with the APR in tiny numbers at the bottom). RUN the program and see if you come up with the same monthly payments as the dealer (the answer in the paper is $170.28 per month).

As it stands, this program is useful enough for straightforward calculation of payments, but a few modifications make it more interesting. First, add this line:

```
100 PRINT "PMT TOTAL=$";N∗P
```

If you run the same numbers through the program, you will find that the payments total is $10,217, which means that you will be paying out a little more than $4,000 worth of interest over the five years. One thing to do with this program is investigate different variations on financing. We will take the case of a hypothetical $8,000 new car and look into some possibilities.

It is possible to make the program call up different choices for the loan terms each time, but we can keep the same short program and take advantage of some features of most small-computer versions of BASIC. One nice touch is that the computer remembers all the old values for variables even outside the program, so that we can change one number at a time and then jump back in for the rest of the calculation. To see how this works, RUN the program with these values: AMOUNT = 8000,

RATE = 20, and MONTHS = 48. This should produce the result

```
PAYMENT PER MONTH=$243.4439
PMT TOTAL=$11685.259
```

Now, what happens if you want to change the rate? Well, as the program has been set up, there is a first block of lines that takes in the information and a second block that does the computing and prints out the summary. A fast way to change one of the loan terms is to set it "externally" and then jump into the program at line 60. Try these lines:

```
LET IX=18
GOTO 60
```

noting that you don't use line numbers here. You should get the display

```
PAYMENT PER MONTH=$235
PMT TOTAL=$11280
```

For further comparison, try these lines also:

```
LET N=60
GOTO 60
```

and you should see the display come up with monthly payments of $203.15 and a total of $12,188.85. This illustrates the general point in auto finance, or any other kind of finance for that matter, that stretching out the payments on the same amount makes a higher total in the end. The increase in the amount paid back is not that bad (after all, the payment term has only been stretched by 25%), but the amount paid out as interest on the whole deal has gone from $3,280 to $4,188.

There is a reasonably simple way to keep all this information on the screen at the same time if you wish. Add these lines:

```
110 PRINT "NEW TERM? Y=1"
120 PRINT "NEW RATE? Y=2"
125 INPUT Y
```

```
130 IF Y=1 THEN GOTO 50
140 IF Y=2 THEN GOTO 200
150 GOTO 300
200 INPUT IX
210 GOTO 60
```

When the program runs through one computation, it now asks if you want to change anything; you respond by giving it the number for your choice, either 1 or 2, and then entering just the new value. If you want to stop the whole show, press in something other than 1 or 2 after the prompt—the program will stop itself. For a fast comparison you might start poking around this question: at 60 months and 20%, the monthly payments were $203 and the total was $12,189. What interest rate would you need on a 48-month loan to get the same monthly payments? With a little searching around you will find the answer to be about 10.2%. The payment total associated with this scheme is, however, a mere $9,776, meaning that you would save about $2,300 over the time the car is financed.

Using the program, we can run through three fast samples of real decisions available from the newspapers.

Dealer interest   If you look closely, you will see that most car dealers offer their lower rates for more "loaded" cars. Compare 48-month financing on a $14,000 car at 9.9% to the same term on a $9,000 car at 13.9%. You will find that the interest on both cars is close to $3,000. This result is one of the reasons that larger cars have not entirely disappeared; they make more money for the auto companies, and in turn the auto companies try to make them easier to buy.

Rebate   If you are offered a $750 rebate on an $8,000 car, should you take the money and run or apply it to the purchase price? At 16% for 60 months on $8,000, the payment total is $11,672, but on $7,250 (using the rebate on purchase), it's only $10,578. The $750 has been worth almost $1000 to you in the long run. If you go for a 48-month term instead, you would end up with nearly the same monthly payments as in the 60-month/$8,000 case, but at 48 months/$7,250 the total works out to $9,862. The rebate has turned into a savings of about $1,800.

Credit unions   Your credit union will go for 90% financing of a new car at 11.5%, or 70% financing of a used car at 15.5% (to these guys, repossession value is a major point). For a 36-month deal, you would end up paying $1,684 in interest charges on a $10,000 new car and $1,437 on an $8,000 used car. So if you want to spend your money on an automobile instead of financing, you may as well get yourself the new car and pray for inflation in the used-car market for later resale.

The short conclusion from these examples is that to the extent that you can afford it, you should plow whatever available money you have into purchasing, rather than borrowing money at high rates. Of course, cars are something of an emotional topic, and it's probably not very satisfying to drive around for years in a car that has only its financing to recommend it. But the program above may help you sift through a few situations from newspaper ads before you go out to look, and thus get the best deal you can come up with on a car you really want.

The Arithmetic of Leasing

Given the economic problems that have afflicted the poor old United States in the last few years, you may at some time have reflected to yourself, quite reasonably, "Who are all these wise guys rolling around in Cadillacs and Jaguars, anyway?" Part of the answer to this searching question may be found in the auto section of the want ads in the newspaper. Here you may cast your eye upon deals that proclaim "New Honda Civic: $149 per month" next to ads that say "New Mercedes 220D: $275 per month." Given that the Mercedes sells for something like six times as much as the Honda, you may wonder why the payments are not six times as much. In wondering this, you have stumbled into the world of leasing; a very great fraction of the expensive steel you see in parking lots is being leased for monthly rates that are lower than the monthly payments on humble family sedans.

How does this work? It is analogous to the balloon-payment scheme in real estate. The dealership or leasing agency that owns the car lends you, in effect, all the money on the cost of the car. It then figures out monthly payments designed to (1) cover the interest part of the loan, and (2) charge an amount that will ultimately cover the depreciation on the vehicle on its way to the used-car lot in three or four years. Thus the classic leasing deal has relatively small payments but a large "residual" at the end of the lease—this residual is the amount you still owe. If the lease has been worked out carefully, the residual should match fairly closely the value of the used car. You then let the dealer sell the car or sell it yourself to cover this debt, and start leasing a new car all over again.

This rather cleanly explains the origins of the expensive steel out in the parking lot. As of mid-1983, a Mercedes 450SL could be counted on to retain 90% of its value over four years. An AMC Concord would retain 44%. Thus the lease, which need only cover depreciation costs, can be quite reasonable for expensive cars that depreciate slowly. If you've got enough money to get into the game, you get to keep it (this is a horrid and unavoidable subtheme in many of these calculations).

For businesses, all the expense of leasing the car can usually be written off taxes as a normal cost of doing business. The business can keep itself in new cars indefinitely without committing cash for down payments (for that matter, it leaves a nice clean nothing to be seized in case of bankruptcy). For individual citizens, the cost of leasing must be allocated between business and personal use. Nonetheless, many people seem to find this convenient compared to outright car ownership. The first thing we will need as a starting point in a discussion of buying versus leasing is a program to work out costs in typical situations.

PROGRAM 4B
Residualism as a Way of Life

```
10 PRINT "ENTER PRICE, RATE"
20 INPUT A
22 INPUT I
25 PRINT A;TAB(10);I
30 PRINT "PMT=?, MONTHS=?"
40 INPUT PX
50 INPUT J
60 PRINT PX;TAB(10);J
70 LET N=60
80 LET I=I/1200
90 LET G=1+I
95 LET RZ=G↑J
100 LET RX=G↑(−N)
110 LET R=(A−PX*(1−RX)/I)*RZ
120 PRINT "RESIDUAL=$";R
```

This program contains two little touches that perhaps should be explained before some examples are run. First, note the use of the TAB function to do some output spacing (consult your computer manual for details on the use of TAB). Second, the real calculation line in this case has been broken up into smaller parts (the parts about RZ and RX). This makes everything easier to type in correctly the first time and easier to change later if necessary.

Starting at the simpler end of things, here is a newspaper example and an analysis of it using the program. The ad says "Honda 1300, $99/mo., cap. cost $5,438, resid. $2,882, 48 mo., $365 drive away." This contains some information you can use right away. The car costs $5,438 and they want $365 down. Between the down payment and 48 monthly payments of $99 dollars, you will have shelled out

$$\$365 + (48 * \$99) = \$5,117$$

on this vehicle, but through the miracle of modern finance you still owe, $2,882. Depending on the lease arrangement, you either pay this amount and keep the car or sell it and turn the money, we hope at least $2,882, over to the leasing agency.

What's the difference between this arrangement and regular purchase payments? For one thing, you will notice that the ad does not state an interest rate (we're going to have to figure that backwards from the numbers). The other difference is that this kind of payment plan is only geared towards bringing down the residual to the projected used-car value. It will turn out that the effective interest rate is about 20%; if you were paying off the car in 48 months under these terms, the payments would be $154 per month. In the leasing case you have paid $2,926 in interest in four years, and in the purchase case $2,319 in interest.

Let's try some numbers in this to see how to work back to the interest rate. Run the program, entering 5438 as PRICE and 16 as a first guess at the rate. PMT will be 99 and MONTHS will be 48. You should get a residual of $1,892, which is too low. A few more attempts at guessing the rate stop at around 20%, which gives a residual of $2,954, close enough for this kind of work. The time base of 60 months as the leasing agency's calculation period is hidden in the calculation in line 70; this seems to be fairly common at the moment, although some leases specifically use longer times.

What emerges from these calculations is the same kind of consideration that applied to interest rates in car loans, that more expensive cars are available at lower rates. Look at this computation of the lease on a BMW 633 CSi, a rather costly little cruiser. This machine lists for $39,545, and the 24-month lease says you can drive this car away for $320 per month. Please observe that this is only about three times as much as the lease on the Honda, while the car itself costs eight times as much. Run the example with these numbers and 16% as the interest rate and you should get back a residual of $36,260. The leasing agency has every reason to expect to be able to sell this creampuff as a used car for several thousand more than that two years from now.

The argument that is presented most strongly for leasing, and one that you will have to mull over for your own tax situation (deductions for cars are somewhat cloudier than, say, for house payments), is that you usually don't have to make much of a down payment. This is stated in one ad the author has seen as "Leasing—for people who have better things to do with their money than drive it around town!" Maybe, and then again maybe not; do you know of something to do with your money that will pay better interest than the 20% the leasing agency is going to charge you? In terms of sheer cost minimization, the cheapest thing to do is pay for the car as fast as possible with the lowest rate you can get, but as has been observed on topics even less emotional than automobiles, there is more to life sometimes than sheer cost minimization.

Getting Out

It may happen that you have an opportunity to get a better financing deal than the one you originally wrote up on your car. You may have financed the car through the dealership at a high interest rate and now have a chance to get a better rate through your credit union. Perhaps you have recently come into some cash from a bonus on the job or have sold some large item (one suspects that a lot of recreational vehicles are being sold to pay for little cars these days). In any case, you will need to know how much you still owe the original lender. Please note that you can't figure this out just from your payments. That is, when you finance a $6,000 car and calculate that the payment total is almost $10,000, you should realize that you don't owe the lender the whole $10,000 if you can pay off the loan early, since this would amount to the lender collecting interest on money you no longer owe. Check the fine print in your lending contract about prepayment conditions, but you will probably find that the rather vigorous recent intrusion of the federal government into consumer lending has made penalties in this area uncommon.

So how much money do you owe? This is computed in the standard type of car loan using the delightfully named *Rule of 78*. The Rule of 78 is a way of apportioning interest vs. principal in consumer loans; there is a different way of doing this for mortgages.

The Rule and the Program

The magic number 78 arises because it is the sum of the numbers from 1 to 12. The total interest amount on a one-year loan is divided into 78 parts; the first month you are considered to be paying 12/78 of the total interest, and the next month 11/78 of the total interest, until in the last month the interest is only 1/78 of the total for the year.

Take, for example, $1,000 at 20% interest for one year. Over the year the payments must total $1,200, so the payments will be $100 per month. For the first payment, the amount of interest paid is

$$\$200 * (12/78) = \$30.77$$

so the amount of principal paid is $100 − $30.77 = $69.33. The next month the amount of interest in the payment is 11/78 of the total finance charge, and so forth. On the last payment, only $2.56 is finance charge.

The procedure for longer time periods runs along the same lines. Instead of 78, the magic number becomes the sum of numbers from 1 to whatever number of months are specified. For a four-year loan, the number is 1,176 and the factor for the first month is 48, since there are 48 months in four years and 1,176 is the sum of numbers from 1 to 48. If this strikes you as the kind of problem that is easier to do on a computer than on the back of an envelope, you are entirely correct. In paying off the loan, it will be necessary to total the interest and principal up to the payoff point and compare these numbers to figure the "interest rebate," which is the money you save by paying off early. Here is a program that does all the work explicitly.

PROGRAM 4C
Interest Rebates

```
10  PRINT "ENTER TOTAL, RATE"
20  INPUT T
30  INPUT I
35  PRINT T;TAB 10;I
40  PRINT "MONTHS=?"
45  INPUT N
50  LET F=T*I*N/1200
55  PRINT "FIN.CHARGE=";F
60  PRINT "PAYOFF MONTH=?"
65  INPUT M
70  LET P=(T+F)/N
75  LET B=T+F-P*M
80  LET Z=(N-M)*(N-M+1)
85  LET Z=Z/(N*(N+1))
90  LET G=B-Z*F
100 PRINT "PMT=$";P
110 PRINT "PMT.TOTAL=$";P*M
115 PRINT "INT.TOT=$";(1-Z)*F
120 PRINT "PAYOFF AMT=$";G
```

The RATE called for by this program is the so-called add-on interest rate, not the APR; if you have any confusion about this, it is the lower of the two rates quoted. That is, in the example at the beginning of this chapter in which the 12% rate quoted was shown to correspond to 20% APR as the real rate, the rate that this program is using is the 12%. The correct number should be available to you in your loan documents, and this method of computing interest specifically only applies to the type of loans in which you find both these numbers floating around, i.e., consumer installment loans.

Just for drill, let's revive the case of the Buick Skylark that started this chapter. The price was $6,385.74 and the rate called for here is 12% (the APR was 20.13%). Let us suppose that at the end of one year you decide that you don't like the terms anymore and you want to get out of the deal and pay off the lender. How much do you owe? Another point is, how much did you pay in interest in this first year (it's deductible)? Try the program with

TOTAL = 6385.74
RATE = 12
MONTHS = 60
PAYOFF MONTH = 12

You should get back payments of $170.28 (we knew that already), and the interesting data that you have paid $2,043.44 over the year, of which $1,369.27 was interest. This can be seen to be about one-third of the total interest over the life of the loan—that's the whole idea in this arrangement, that the lender gets his interest out fast. The bottom line, so to speak, in this example, is that you need $5,711.57 to buy out of the original financing.

So what you have to consider, if you want to explore alternative financing, is what your payments will be on $5,711.57 (if you let the original deal stand, you will end up paying $8,173.44, which is just four more years of payments at $170.28). In practice, this will work out to require that you find financing with a lower real rate (or lower APR) than about 18% in this case. Given that a reasonable spread in the credit market is about 5% from the best rates to the worst, this shouldn't be too tough.

There is also the qualitative conclusion that, if you want to do something about a consumer loan, you should do it as close to the beginning as possible. Take the example of a $10,000 loan at 12% add-on interest. We will use 60 months as the term and think about jumping out after three years (36 months). Try these numbers and you should find:

PMT=$266.67 per month
FIN. CHARGE=$6,000
INT. TOT=$5,016.39 to date
PAYOFF AMT=$5,416.39

You still owe $5,416.39, but the remaining payments, if you keep the same loan, will be 24*$266.67=$6,400. The equivalent real interest rate for doing better than this works out to about 16%, but in fact even a few hundred dollars in loan cost would mean that you would have to find a deal at 14% or better. Thus, if you want to have misgivings about this kind of finance, the time to do it is probably near the first-year mark rather than at the end.

This survey suggests that once you decide on a car that you want, comparison-shopping loan possibilities will probably do you hundreds or thousands of dollars' worth of good when you actually buy. One thing you might like to do is make up a little table of monthly payments and payment totals based on the rates available to you from different lenders. You will be thrilled with the amount of respect you get at banks and car dealerships if you obviously have some idea of how car payments work; these people are used to dealing with consumers who just have to take all payment information on faith. And that is why all these cheap computers are such a jolly business; you can figure out anything the bank can figure out!

5
Housing and Related Problems

Housing, once upon a time, was not quite the problem it has become recently. In 1955 or so, it was possible to buy a nice $10,000 house and finance it for twenty-five years at 4% interest. This worked out to give house payments of about $53 per month. The same house, using the averages for California at any rate, now sells for $87,000 and the interest rate for a mortgage now runs between 10% and 16%, depending on the whims of the Federal Reserve Board. This means payments of $790 to $1,180 per month, and even making a generous inflation adjustment, it is clear that families are spending a much larger fraction of their income on housing than was formerly the case. It is not much consolation that some areas of the United States have escaped some of the worst of this house price explosion; these have typically been places like Detroit and other industrial cities whose industries are in poor health.

Prices are certainly higher in general than they were in the 1950s, but on most items in the budget the factor is four or five times higher, not *twenty* times higher as is the case for housing.

This problem has its roots in two fairly novel situations. First, the population of the United States has, and will have for decades to come, an odd distribution by age because of the notorious baby boom after World War II. When this flood of population reached home-buying age in markets that were already tight, prices climbed at a very discouraging rate—discouraging at least to the prospective home buyers. Second, the last few years have seen an economic process in America that for lack of a better word may be called "Europeanization." After World War II, the United States was the only industrial nation in reasonable economic shape; Americans drove big cars with V-8 engines and ate steak for dinner while Europeans drove tiny cars and made their own pasta. Now that America is just one big country in an economic world with many other major countries, Americans get to drive small cars and figure out what wine to have with quiche at brunch. The food may be better, but the bad news for real estate in Europeanization is that the way Europeans get to own homes is that they have to save like crazy, work all sorts of deals, wait for their parents to die, or just get stuck renting forever anyway. Not too many cottages with white picket fences in the suburbs in Italy, for example.

Europeans, however, do not face the peculiar tax laws that make owning your own real estate so important in the United States. Here interest payments on loans, in this case home-mortgage loans, are tax-deductible. There are two compelling features of this arrangement: first, the mortgage payment is usually larger than all other legitimate deductions these days, so the house payment is one of the few unquestioned avenues to a lower tax bracket; second, it is one of the few straightforward deductions on necessities rather than items of choice. For example, if you can work out an excuse, your computer is tax-deductible. But, with all due respect, you could probably live without it, so the deductibility just amounts to a discount. The value of your discount is the percentage of your income that you pay in taxes (if you don't know this number offhand, go find it out now—you'll need it soon). House payments, on the other hand, represent money you were probably going to have to spend on living accommodations anyway, so the deduction is notably more valid. Just think, if you could deduct food, clothes, and movie tickets, you'd be in great shape! Basically, the deduction of the interest part of house payments is the only tax break for average wage-earning citizens.

This chapter contains a variety of general-purpose

programs, some of which will become more and some less necessary depending on conditions. What is likely to occur during the life of this book (we're assuming that by 1990 you won't need books like this because you will be able to buy a voice-input computer with a one-inch, 400-megabyte hard disk that programs in English for $29.99) is this: (1) the main lump of baby-boom population will pass through the housing market, creating local price explosions wherever the jobs are; (2) the government will use interest rates to control inflation, so that refinancing will be going on every time rates go down; (3) every time political trouble elsewhere in the world hits countries with a fair-sized wealthy class (Iran was a great example), money will flood into the real-estate market of the dear old stable USA, creating temporary booms. Ideally, what you would like to do is stick some poor bank with a twenty-year fixed-interest loan at 5%, but it may reasonably be feared that this rare honor was reserved for all time to the veterans of World War II.

So we plunge onward into the new world of nearly constant finagling and scheming, aided in this quest by a computer that costs between $12 and $80 in 1955 money. You win some, you lose some. For convenience, here is a short directory of the programs for this chapter:

Program 5A: Plain Payments

This is just the straightforward computation of PMT from total price and the finance terms, with prompts put in so that input and output don't require much concentration. This is necessary because residents of either coast will probably want to have drinks in their hands to be able to countenance the bottom line.

Program 5B: Buying vs. Renting

This program retranslates the amount of house payments into an equivalent rent, taking the tax situation of the prospective homeowner into account. This is a country in which, in general, landlords have more influence on tax laws than renters do.

Program 5C: Refinancing

Almost the only program in the book that involves pro-gramming with the IF statement, this allows repeated com-putation, changing one term (e.g., interest) at a time. Com-parisons of different deals are thus left on the screen.

Program 5D: Balloon Payments

Many homeowners are faced with refinancing short-term loans that culminate in a balloon payment, and some of these balloons are gigantic. This program shows how bal-loons are computed and compares different approaches to take when the payment is due.

Program 5E: The Inflatable House

The only attractive part of thirty-year mortgages is the prospect of paying back the bank in over-inflated funny-money as the years go by. The bank, of course, knows this and wants to charge you an interest rate at least a few points ahead of inflation (one reason for the variable-interest-rate mortgage). This program estimates what the real total of your home loan payments will be, considering different prospects for long-term inflation or deflation.

Starting Point

You will find this hard to believe, after typing in the follow-ing short program, but you can buy something like this as a "software package," on floppy disk no less, in one case for $49.95 for the Apple II Plus. It has been asked by different skeptics, "How often do you want to calculate your mortgage?" The answer to this is that you may want to check out a few alternatives from time to time, and a piece of good advice may certainly be worth $50, but it is certainly nice to be able to do this work on a computer with just a cassette drive and a price in many cases under $100.

Here is the simplest form of a payment program:

PROGRAM 5A
Plain Payments

```
10 PRINT "AMOUNT=?"
15 INPUT T
20 PRINT T
25 PRINT "RATE=?"
30 INPUT IX
35 PRINT IX
40 PRINT "YEARS=?"
45 INPUT NY
50 PRINT NY
55 LET I=IX/1200
58 LET F=1+I
60 LET N=NY*12
65 LET P=T*I/(1−F↑(−N))
70 PRINT "PMT=$";P
75 PRINT "TOTAL=$";P*N
```

Even a program as simple as this contains some interesting messages. Try entering 60000 for the amount, 16 for the rate, and 30 for the number of years. You should be rewarded with the straightforward response

```
PMT=$806.85
TOTAL=$290467.51
```

This may be straightforward, but it's not especially encouraging; $60,000 is not a whopping sum to finance these days, but $800 is a pretty serious payment for an average family (the metropolitan-area average family of four having less than $20,000 per year gross income). The problem is aggravated by the tendency of banks to try to be obliging about payments and lower them by extending the pay-back period. Run the program with the same numbers, except use forty years as the term. You should see:

```
PMT=$801.39
TOTAL=$384666.77
```

Admittedly, this is an extreme example, but it makes a point. The point is that extending the payment period always increases the ultimate cost of a mortgage by an enormous amount. Lengthening the time from thirty years to forty years results in essentially no reduction in payments but boosts the total by nearly $100,000. For reference, the payments on a twenty-year term would be $834.75, with a total of $200,340.86; on fifteen years, payments are $881.22 and the total is $158,619.67. Amazingly enough, when you go into a bank for a mortgage, they will begin writing it up for whatever standard term is current but frequently have no objection to making the term shorter—you just have to know enough to ask! Remember also that unless the inflation rate is outrunning the mortgage interest rate (something that is politically unlikely on a time scale of decades), the fact that the later payments are worth less in constant dollars doesn't reverse the advantage of shorter term loans. There is a tactic you can use that essentially shortens your loan period; it will be discussed in the next chapter in the section on IRAs.

Rental Economics

Suppose for a moment you have succeeded in scrounging up some sort of down payment towards purchasing a home, or have worked out a "creative" deal in which you are going to be able to borrow the down payment and will be making monthly payments on the whole package. It is of considerable importance, both to yourself and to the lenders involved, to determine what sort of payments you can stand without withering from the pain. These payments will be higher than the rental payments you have been making, because the new payments will be tax-deductible (at the beginning of a long-term mortgage the payments are almost pure interest). The question is: Exactly how much can you afford without finding yourself much worse off in monthly economy than you were before getting into your new real estate?

The following program will give an approximate guideline for figuring what mortgage payment you can afford, given the level of rent you are accustomed to paying. It assumes that the house payments are your principal new tax deduction, makes an estimate of the tax break (including the effect of dropping to a lower bracket), and resolutely ignores insurance and property tax. These last two you should find out for yourself and subtract from the number the computer gives you. It should be emphasized that this is a very conservative approach—there is no assumption that you are willing to scrimp and save any more vigorously than you were while you were renting. In practice, this kind of estimate is much less likely to get you into trouble; remember, when things go wrong in the new place, you pay for it, not the landlord (houses can be expensive in novel and mysterious ways). Type in this program and we'll try some examples:

PROGRAM 5B
Buying vs. Renting

```
10 PRINT "RENT=?"
15 INPUT R
20 PRINT R
30 PRINT "INCOME=?, TAXES=?"
35 INPUT M
40 INPUT T
45 PRINT M;TAB 10;T
50 LET V=T/M
55 LET MX=R*12*(1+V)
60 LET Y=.043*MX/10000
65 LET VN=V−Y
70 LET TN=(M−MX)*VN
75 LET P=R+(T−TN)/12
80 PRINT "PMT LEVEL=$";P
```

This contains the approximation in line 60 that you are married and filing a joint return (this has to do with bracket scaling). If you are single, you can change the numerical factor in this line from .043 to .052 for more accurate results. Since this contains the assumption that all your other deductions have stayed the same, the results are only to be taken as guidelines (but they're pretty close guidelines).

Let's enter the case of two people bringing in $32,000 per year, who paid $6,100 in taxes, and are currently shelling out $450 per month in rent (all the tragic cases in this section are actual sad stories of friends of the author). An equivalent mortgage level for these folks turns out to be $611; this is fairly encouraging—it would be the payments on a $60,000 mortgage at 12% (thirty years).

Somewhat farther down the income scale, try the example of a couple paying $380 in rent, with an income of $21,000 and taxes of $3,100. The program says that their equivalent mortgage level is about $474; that is, they can afford a mortgage payment approximately 25% higher than the rent payment. But the tax laws are set up to provide the greatest benefits to people a little better off than these modest citizens. If you double the income level, to $42,000, you get taxes of $9,900 or so from the tables. Punch in $760 for rent and see what happens. The program should give a payment level of $1,105 for the equivalent mortgage; that's 46% higher than the rent level. The moral of this short computational tale (please put in your own case for a personal touch) is that if you are making more than $35,000 on a joint return, in 1982 dollars, the tax laws will give you tremendous assistance in buying a house. Keep in mind that the payment level suggested by this program is for all house-related, mostly-interest payments. At this rate you could take out a separate loan from some source for a down payment and still manage an average house in most of the U.S. If you don't have as much income, things are not so wonderful, but there is still a substantial effect down to $16,000 per year. This effect is why home ownership is such a critical business in America, while many Europeans are quite happy to rent apartments forever.

Finance Choices

This program is designed to allow you to recompute payments under a variety of conditions and keep them on screen for comparison. Because of constraints on space (these programs are designed to fit in minimal RAM, about 1K, and be easy to type in), there are some external calculations to perform, but these will be explained as we go along. At the time this program was first written, interest rates for mortgages were topped out and had been static for almost a year; when rates began dropping, there was in one week a four-point spread available from different banks. This sort of thing has prospects of going on forever, so this program may be more useful than originally imagined. Here is the program listing:

PROGRAM 5C
Refinancing

```
 10 PRINT "ENTER:AMT,RATE,YRS"
 20 INPUT A
 30 INPUT R
 40 INPUT Y
 50 PRINT "AMT=$";A
 60 PRINT "RATE=";R
 70 PRINT "YEARS=";Y
 80 LET N=Y*12
 90 LET I=R/1200
100 LET P=A*I/(1-(1+I)↑(-N))
110 PRINT "PAYMENT=$";P
120 PRINT "CHANGE? AM=1,RT=2,YR S=3,NO=4"
130 INPUT D
132 IF D=1 THEN INPUT A
134 IF D=2 THEN INPUT R
136 IF D=3 THEN INPUT Y
138 IF D=4 THEN GOTO 180
140 GOTO 50
```

The amount referred to here is the loan total, which includes points and loan fees. You can either add these up separately or do the arithmetic in the input line. For example, $50,000 plus one and a half points plus a $550 loan fee would be entered as

        50000*(1.015)+550

where the "points" are entered in the factor in parentheses (the points are just percentage points of the original amount added on). One use of this program is to draw up a little table, changing one value at a time. Let us take a loan for $75,000 total amount and see what happens for a thirty-year loan at 10, 12, 14, and 16%. This should produce these results:

        10%:   PAYMENT=$658.18
        12%:   PAYMENT=$771.46
        14%:   PAYMENT=$888.65
        16%:   PAYMENT=$1008.57

The immediate conclusion you may draw from this is that anytime the rates drop more than about two points lower than those of your original mortgage, you should seriously consider rewriting it. Worst-case loan fees and points will be at most a few thousand dollars; this means you would in principle save money if your payments went down only a few dollars per month (remember that a thirty-year mortgage means 360 payments). The only practical matter here is timing. You don't want to do this too often, since you do incur finance charges every time you change your paperwork, so you will have to guess when rates are at a temporary low point.

Sixty Months in a Balloon: Adventures in High Finance

In rising real-estate markets there is a pronounced tendency for lenders to be willing to write short-term (five- or ten-year) loans with large balloon payments at the end.

The principle here is really much like auto leasing; it presents a way to arrive at low monthly payments, by the expedient of simply not attempting to pay anything on the loan other than interest. The hope implicit in this sort of paperwork is that when the balloon comes due, several things may be possible: (1) the house has risen in price to the point where the owners can clear out and pay off the loan at an immense profit, chuckling all the way to the bank, or; (2) interest rates have fallen to the point where normal long-term house financing doesn't result in impossible payments, or; (3) another balloon can be sent up until either (1) or (2) occurs.

Sometimes this works out and sometimes it doesn't. The thinking behind most balloon financing can be summarized in a very old and very profound joke (the only joke in this book, believe it or not; everything else is serious). It seems the King of France is passing through a village where a man is about to be hanged for horse thievery and, following the custom of the times, decides to pull up a chair and watch. As the thief is being led to the gallows, he spots the king and cries out, "Sire, I am unjustly accused—I was just borrowing the horse to teach it to talk!" The king is intrigued by this and has the man brought to him. The king hears his story and gives him two years to teach the king's favorite horse to talk, with the threat that he is to be trampled to death slowly by the same horse if the experiment doesn't work. The horse thief goes back and tells the story to his friends, who tell him he is crazy to pass up a nice, clean hanging in favor of such a messy demise. The thief replies, "Listen, my friends, in two years many things can happen. I might get sick and die anyway. The king is old and he might die also. Or the horse might run away. Or the horse might die. Or, the horse might talk!"

This program calculates the payments for a given value of the balloon, using standard real-estate-loan practice. The loan is usually written as a thirty-year amortization, with the balloon due after a shorter period. It has been common practice in rising real-estate markets to make the balloon equal to the whole amount borrowed.

PROGRAM 5D
Balloon Payments

```
10 PRINT "AMT=?,BALLOON=?"
15 INPUT T
20 INPUT B
25 PRINT T;TAB 10;B
30 PRINT "MONTHS=?, RATE=?"
35 INPUT J
40 INPUT IX
45 PRINT J;TAB 10;IX
50 LET I=IX/1200
55 LET A=(1-(1+I)↑(-360))/I
60 LET P=T-B*(1+I)↑(-J)
65 LET P=P/A
70 PRINT "PMT=$";P
```

Try this out with the following numbers: AMT = 49500, BALLOON = 49500, MONTHS = 60, and RATE = 16. This should give you $365 (rounded to the nearest dollar) for payments. This example, drawn from a painful episode in real life, illustrates the point about the talking horse: the loan was taken out in the hope that the house price would go up considerably in the five years of the loan. In fact the house price dropped slightly, so that the net effect to the homeowner was a cash loss (not to mention the money spent on the loan, which, with a 100% balloon as in this case, is an example of "renting your house from the bank"). With a thirty-year mortgage, the possibility of getting away with the deal is considerably greater; with a five-year balloon, your real-estate judgment has to be pretty astute. Horses just don't learn to talk that fast.

But the reason people go for this kind of arrangement is not hard to find. By running the same example using balloon=0, you can determine the cost of monthly payments for the usual mortgage scheme. This number turns out to be $665.65, and the difference of $300 per month is in many families the difference between eating and not eating (or at least not getting into the house).

Balloon arrangements can lead to some very odd trade-offs in the way of easy payments vs. larger long-run costs. Try the example of $100,000 with a 10-year 100% balloon, at 18% interest. You should come up with payments of $1,254.61; this may be compared to $1,507.08 for the regular thirty-year payments with no balloon. For a two-year period instead of the ten years, the payments are about $453. This is one of the reasons why balloon arrangements are typical in the financing of new businesses—if the business is expected to grow, the balloon scheme conserves working capital in the critical first stages of the business. It is hoped, if the money spared in this way is plowed into advertising or production, there will be no problem with regular financing when the balloon comes due. But this procedure is something of a gamble, and it is not much less of a gamble when private housing is involved instead of business.

Time Is on Your Side (Perhaps)

The years since World War II have been characterized by a gradual but persistent rise in price level. This frequently gives people the impression that things were delightfully cheap in the good old days; in fact, the average industrial wage in the United States has been fairly close to two cartons of cigarettes per hour for decades now (all discussions of the prices in the good old days should be required to start by renormalizing wage levels to the price of goods; the Model T was not really such an incredible bargain as is often suggested).

This situation is not necessarily the only way things can be. There have been many deflationary periods in U.S. economic history and in the history of most countries. There have also been periods of decades in which the price level has remained constant. But there are several reasons for believing that the next few decades will not be deflationary, assuming of course that we are not all blasted to eternity defending our national honor (the author took a macroeconomics course once from a professor who had a grant to formulate a model of prices after World War III, a curious exercise to say the least . . . gasoline and shotgun shells were rather costly). First, there is an inflationary pressure created by depletion of stocks of raw materials. Although the price of oil, for example, may fluctuate downwards for a few years at a time, it is difficult to imagine petroleum getting steadily cheaper year after year. Second, it turns out to be easier for a central bank, such as the U.S. Federal Reserve System, to manage and control mild inflation than other types of economic situations. The modern banking system already has its procedures in place for dealing with inflation, as long as it is not absolutely runaway, and there is a persistent prejudice that some inflation is actually healthy, i.e., encourages consumption and entrepreneurial optimism. Whether these reasons are flaming nonsense or not, there are more institutions with a vested interest in inflation than deflation at the moment, so this is the topic we will pursue.

The program here calculates the total of payments on a real-estate loan in nominal dollars and compares it to the value in constant dollars. If the inflation rate is zero, these numbers will be the same. If the inflation rate is enormous, the payments in constant dollars thirty years from now will of course be approximately zilch. A more interesting approach, perhaps, than using the straight inflation rate is to use a rate that reflects what your salary increases are likely to be; this gives you a "difficulty" index on the payments. That is, if the inflation rate is 8% and your raise is more likely to be 6%, plugging in 6% is going to tell you how hard it will be for you personally to make the payments.

PROGRAM 5E
The Inflatable House

```
10 PRINT "AMT=?,RATE=?"
15 INPUT T
20 INPUT IX
25 LET I=IX/1200
30 PRINT T;TAB 10;IX
```

```
40 PRINT "INFLATION=?"
45 INPUT X
50 PRINT X
55 LET Z=1—X/1200
60 LET N=360
65 LET W=T*I/(1—(1+I)↑(—N))
70 LET Q=W*(1—Z↑N)/(1—Z)
75 PRINT "TOTAL=$";W*N
80 PRINT "CONST.TOT=$";Q
```

We may as well try this for a benchmark amount, say $10,000, at 12% interest and a background of 6% inflation. The program should give the result:

```
TOTAL=$370300.54
CONST.TOT=$171870.01
```

You may want to try the constant-dollar amount for different inflation rates; for example, at 16% the constant total is only $76,531.23, which is less than the amount you borrowed. This example is pretty unlikely, since the social structure of the U.S. would probably have gotten quite strange in the course of thirty years of that kind of inflation.

It is possible to poke around in this program and find out some interesting things. At 8% the constant-dollar total is $140,406.87, which does not seem like much of a contrast to the 6% case (although the last payment is a heartwarming $92.57 in constant dollars, compared to $1,028.61 at the start). The reason for this is that mortgage payments load all the interest payment near the beginning, so the bank gets back its money fairly fast as a hedge against long-term inflation. Another point to consider is historical: for many years the banks charged interest rates that were 2 or 3% above the inflation rate. These days, it appears that 5 or 6% above inflation is a standard formula, with higher rates likely (for 1982 the inflation rate was running around 4 or 5% and the home loan rate rarely dropped below 13). It is good to know what the real cost of a loan is, but it is even better (as we will see in the next chapter) to be able to do something about it.

6
Savings, Cash Management, and Retirement

These topics are grouped together because, although at first glance they have little in common, they are linked by two rather powerful similarities. The main point is that they all concern conserving your own cash rather than working out payments to someone else. A secondary point is that all the schemes to be evaluated—for example, money-market checking accounts, IRAs, and high-interest time deposits—are all products of a new wave of banking services that are really fairly recent. The 1970s and 1980s have seen a virtual explosion in the number of devices that banks have thought up to lure investors, after decades of offering savings accounts with pathetically low returns. As your Social Awareness Self-Test No. 1, you might like to try this question: Which organizations do you think lobbied for the laws that told the banks to pay such low interest for all those years, hmmm?

There is no question that the new banking devices have attracted billions of dollars in new deposits, prying some savings at last out of the most reluctant industrial country in the world at saving. Presumably the banks can now go out and make judicious loans to worthy enterprises and individuals. Also, it certainly wouldn't hurt most large American international banks to have a little extra cash on hand in case some of their ill-considered loans to developing Third World countries, made in a spirit of optimism in the late 1970s, go terminally sour as a result of upheaval or simple inability to make even the interest payments. (If you start to read in the papers about Mexico or Poland deciding to send their sad regrets to Citibank, you may consider all advice in this chapter to be no longer applicable and you should try to get yourself a few acres in the country to grow vegetables, keep a few chickens, and watch at a distance to see how it all turns out.)

The decisions that go into this chapter may be considered with special care because they concern only financial instruments. In the chapter on consumer loans, there were perhaps noncomputable factors that could influence a decision; for example, you could just want a new TV right now more than life itself, or you could decide that saving one cent per day to buy a new refrigerator would be an inspiring Zen activity, but in the cases in this chapter there is only pure money, and the assumption will be prominent that you want as much of it as you can get.

Before plunging into computation, it is worth noting that all these considerations about savings are only possible when the value of the currency is reasonably stable. In the Israeli economy, for example, the idea of cash savings is utter nonsense. The inflation rate in Israel has been higher than 100% for many years; as a result, people try to put their savings into foreign currencies or into stock shares, which tend to be self-indexing for inflation. (The Israeli system assumes that basic wages are already indexed, but the price increases are so rapid that it is a normal situation that everyone's checking account will be overdrawn by the end of the month and the banks just lend overdraft money at incredible rates). The notion of savings in paper money is really quite a novelty in world history and is still rare outside mature industrial economies. Rampant paranoia is not necessarily in order, but long-term savings plans might judiciously take into account that political matters can have a great impact on economics. For example, Mexico recently handed many of its citizens the sad news that their bank accounts were henceforth to be worth only a fraction of their former value; under those circumstances an old box full of Taxco silver would be a better bet than paper pesos, no matter what the computer thinks.

The programs here will attempt to be general enough to be useful, and fortunately, banking laws change slowly enough that most of this material should age acceptably.

Actually, if you have read the first few chapters and this one as well, you will have seen fairly clearly that *all* financial calculations fall into a small number of classes. Just a little modification of input and output of these programs should be sufficient to update them, whatever fabulous new deals the financial institutions see fit to offer the eager public. As it happens, the mathematics of saving is simpler than the mathematics of time payment of debt, so the programs are all quite short.

This is a directory of programs:

6A: Simple Savings
6B: Regular Deposits
6C: Zero Coupons
6D: Simple Savings/Tax/Inflation
6E: IRA Accounts

Straight-Time Deposits

The simplest program possible computes the result of depositing money at interest for a given amount of time. Even this program has some distinctly educational features, however, as we shall see.

PROGRAM 6A
Simple Savings

```
10 PRINT "RATE=?,DEP=?"
15 INPUT IX
20 INPUT D
25 PRINT IX;TAB 10;D
30 PRINT "TERM(YRS)"
35 INPUT NY
40 LET N=NY*365
45 LET I=IX/36500
50 LET T=D*(1+I)↑N
55 PRINT "BAL=$";T
```

This is the appropriate form for simple passbook savings. One of the first things you will notice is that the middle section of the program is a little different from earlier work; the compounding period is one day rather than one month, so that 365s pop up where there have usually been 12s. Now when you try this program for a particular test set—use DEP=100 and RATE=5.25 (the standard passbook rate)—you will see why this business is always phrased as "5¼% (5.39% annual yield)." The effect of chopping the original 5¼% interest into 365 tiny chunks and compounding them produces a slightly higher effective rate. This compounding effect results in an even larger annual yield, compared to the original rate, for higher starting interest.

The reason this is worth noting is that for starting interest rates near 10% the effect is worth about 1%, and it happens that most fixed-time deposits are paid on a simple-interest basis rather than compounded. Make sure you note what yield you are actually getting when you make the deposit (by law it has to be stated, it just doesn't necessarily have to be stated so that it is obvious to you if you don't know what you're doing). There are also some other minor peculiarities in this work—most money-market time deposits use 360 days instead of 365 as the compounding cycle, but this won't change things significantly.

Dedicated Savings

You may decide to have a payroll savings plan or some form of automatic saving at regular intervals, usually monthly. There are several ways to do the calculation, but the one that results in the most convenient program is shown here.

PROGRAM 6B
Regular Deposits

```
10 PRINT "RATE=?, MO.DEP.=?"
15 INPUT IX
20 INPUT D
25 PRINT IX;TAB 10;D
```

```
30 PRINT "MONTHS=?"
33 INPUT N
36 PRINT N
40 LET Y=(1+IX/36500)↑365
45 LET Z=EXP((LOG(Y))/12)
50 LET T=D*(1-Z↑N)/(1-Z)
55 PRINT "TOTAL=$";T
```

When you type in this program, please note two points. First, you can make a tape copy of Program 6A and recall it and save yourself about half the typing work by using part of the old program. Second, observe that EXP and LOG are functions you may or may not be familiar with, but this program will do just fine whether you understand it or not. What's going on here is that for convenience the program makes up a monthly rate that gives the same value as compounding daily.

Let us try a few examples of diligent saving. Use 5.25 as the interest rate and 100 as the monthly deposit; run this for one, two, and three years. This should allow you to make up this table for the totals:

Months	Balance
12	$1,229.36
24	$2,524.99
36	$3,890.44

You will note that at the end of the first year you will have earned the magnificent total of $29.36 as interest earnings for your efforts (that's before taxes, anyway). Please observe that if you were to owe $1,000 on a typical credit card, the interest charge for *one month* would be $15. Thus it may be concluded that if you are in a position to have any money regularly extracted from your paycheck, it should go towards debt reduction rather than savings. Perhaps you might think that this wouldn't need to be pointed out to anyone; nonetheless, it happens that millions of people in the United States are faithfully paying into a savings plan every month while they make sporadic or minimum payments on credit-card debts and consumer loans. Saving money at 5.25% and paying interest at 20% will certainly keep the bank managers whistling as they stroll to lunch, but it won't do you much good.

A (Relatively) New Savings Plan

One curious new instrument (or financial product, as the wise men in marketing like to call it) for saving is the zero coupon. In this plan you buy a note, much like an old-time U.S. Savings Bond, for some modest amount and then hold it for, typically, five or ten years. These are rather odd in the sense that you will find yourself being taxed on interest that you can't collect until the note comes due; on the other hand, they are fairly close to ideal as a gift to children (for founding a college fund—if your kids are already paying taxes on their incomes, you don't need this book) or as something to dump into your IRA, if you have decided you want one (this way the interest doesn't get taxed, at least not yet). The interesting computation is the starting price. The notes are usually set out in $1,000 values, with the choice of five years or ten years for a term. This program computes the price you will have to pay to buy the note (worth $1,000 at maturity).

PROGRAM 6C
Zero Coupons

```
10 PRINT "RATE=?, YRS=?"
15 INPUT IX
20 INPUT NY
25 PRINT IX;TAB 10;NY
30 LET N=NY*365
35 LET I=IX/36500
40 LET P=1000/((1+I)↑N)
50 PRINT "PRICE=$";P
```

Try this for 10.5% interest and 10 years. You should find that the coupon costs $350 (rounded off). This is interesting for several reasons. These notes, first of all, are the only way people with modest amounts of money can get in on relatively high interest rates. It also represents a form of speculation on both interest rates and inflation, since in locking up your money for ten years you are betting that the rate on the zero coupon will be better than both of these percentages over the whole ten years.

This brings up a rather serious question, namely, is it possible to figure out an optimal savings scheme with ordinary bank options by using the computer? It is possible, but it depends on probabilistic estimates of the range of interest rates over the savings period. After consideration of the economic history of the last ten years, it appears that the best deal from the point of view of minimizing risk and maximizing yield is that offered by time deposits from 91 days to one year. Basically, if you don't have an amount of money you can set aside for at least 91 days, you're not really into this game anyway. Conversely, it is very difficult to determine what rate is fair in return for, say, locking up your money for three to ten years.

As an illustration of the sort of strange things that can happen under current plans (circa 1982), consider the so-called money-market checking account. A fairly standard variant of these requires a $2,500 minimum deposit and specifies that the interest rate drops to 5¼% with a monthly service charge of $5 on balances below $2,500. This means that you will in practice be earning less than 3% if you let the average balance in the account dip below $2,500 during any month. Thus, unless you are sure that you won't need the money, this is not actually such an exceptional prospect; if you *are* sure you won't need the money, you can usually find a better return in a different account, usually a fixed-time deposit.

Real Yield

The remarkable tax laws of the United States dictate that earned interest is taxable while interest payments you must make are tax-deductible. The result of this is of course to reduce effective yield on savings according to your tax bracket. Furthermore, the interest earnings are taxed as if they were real money, with no adjustment for inflation; so the true yield is worse yet. We will look at a short program that estimates this effective yield, and then think about what can be done.

PROGRAM 6D
Simple Savings/Tax/Inflation

```
10 PRINT "INT.RATE=?"
15 INPUT IX
20 PRINT IX
25 PRINT "INFLATION=?"
30 INPUT F
35 PRINT F
40 PRINT "TAX RATE=?"
45 INPUT R
50 PRINT R; " PERCENT"
55 LET Y=1−F/100
60 LET Z=1−R/100
65 LET B=Y*(1+IX*Z)
68 LET B=100*B
70 PRINT "YIELD PER $100=";B
```

A few comments are in order. First, the interest rate asked for in this program is the effective annual yield (i.e., 5.39% for 5.25% annual rate). If you wish, you can use the program line

```
28 LET IX=((1+IX/365000)↑365)−1
```

which will convert ordinary rates like 5.25 to their annual-yield equivalent, but usually you will have the annual-yield information anyway. Second, the tax information should be your total taxes divided by your gross income; this will reflect how much of the interest you will pay in taxes unless your interest income is a large fraction of your total income (in which case you are presumably rich, and should be having your accountant do this figuring for you). You may use the published consumer price index for inflation, and it wouldn't hurt to kick in an extra point or two for realism, as this figure has had rather a lot of politics stirred into it lately. Many government benefits are indexed to this number, and the government therefore has a vested interest in undercomputing it.

Try this program for 5.39% interest, a 20% tax bracket, and inflation rates of 4% and 8%. You should get the answers

Inflation	Yield
4%	$100.14
8%	$ 95.97

What makes this especially unpleasant is that the annual yield of 5.39% on ordinary passbook savings is a number that the banking industry has succeeded in engraving in stone forever, whereas an annual inflation rate of 4% is very nearly the best economic performance of the last decade, if indeed the figure can be trusted. Although, of course, inflation will be eating up your money even more rapidly if you bury it in a jar in the backyard, it is nonetheless pretty discouraging to observe that with any realistic estimate of the inflation rate, you will be losing money in real terms at ordinary bank rates. This, among other reasons, is why financial advisers invariably suggest something other than regular old savings as a place for your money.

This program also explains why a brief perusal of the business section of the newspaper or magazines about money management gives evidence of great activity in state and municipal bonds. If you are in a tax bracket approaching 50%, and more people are these days as a result of "bracket creep," there is essentially no bank savings plan that will do you any good. Even money-market schemes that pay 12% or so are going to be unattractive, since after taxes you only get 6% and still have inflation to face. Careful shopping around will show some tax-free bond issues that have yields of 65% or so of the highest time-deposit rates; this not only works out to give you more interest if you're in such a high bracket, but typically the rates will be locked for a long period. A promising new scheme is the variable-rate municipal bond, which is a virtual guarantee that you will always get a better yield than you could get elsewhere. The problem with most of these plans is that they require a large minimum deposit, but if you find yourself in the 50% bracket, you certainly should be able to come up with a decent lump sum at some point (or at least you won't find too many ordinary citizens who sympathize).

Into the Sunset

People have some very strange ideas about retirement. When the Prussian State Civil Service invented the retirement age of sixty-five in the last century, it was confidently assumed that the retiree would have the good grace to drop in his tracks within a year or two after his farewell party. Now somehow it is imagined that one should be able to retire at sixty-five, live for twenty more years, get all medical expenses covered by the government, and that all this will have been taken care of by tiny contributions during the working career. It *can't* actually be made to work this way, and like so many things that can't happen, it doesn't.

Consider a point of very simple arithmetic. Suppose there were no taxes and no inflation, and you were able to save 10% of your income for a retirement fund. What this means is that for every ten years you work, you will be able to retire *for one year* on an amount equal to your average working salary. If you want to retire at sixty-five, you had better plan to take up skydiving or something around your sixty-eighth birthday, because you will be able to see the end, of your funds at least, rapidly approaching. You would also be wise to avoid ever becoming ill.

One can hear absolutely remarkable arguments from

older people these days about the amount of money they feel they must have paid into the Social Security system over the years. In fact, the average Social Security pensioner recovers his entire contribution in about two years or so after retirement (this is roughly in accord with the unforgiving arithmetic of the preceding paragraph).

The money paid into the system has in fact all been spent manys times over, and the whole operation is fueled by current contributions and an increasing tendency to encroach on tax revenues. This is not necessarily because of government mismanagement, as is often sourly claimed. The two principal problems are really: (1) an unanticipated enthusiasm of the WW II generation for leaving work early, and (2) the impact of inflation, against which no savings-pension plan can hope to stand.

Another problem is that there are nowhere near enough new young workers entering the labor force to keep this pumping along comfortably. Social Security payroll tax by the early 1980s has risen past 10%; by the year 2000 it will have to be 28% and by 2020, 40% to maintain the current level of benefits. The population statistics demand this as the ratio of retired persons to active workers steadily increases. To be frank, the author expects that his daughter would take to the hills in a guerrilla movement against old folks before she would countenance turning over half her paycheck every month so Daddy could work on his tennis game at Sun City. Something's got to give, and everybody who studies these matters knows it.

In an effort to forestall the impending crunch, the government came up with a plan called the Individual Retirement Account, or IRA. These have become phenomenally popular as a result of a widespread belief that they are a wonderful form of tax shelter (whether this is true or not will be the subject of some computation). Another reason for their popularity is the belief, voiced by a number of cynical and not-so-cynical observers, that the government is simply going to call off Social Security for most of the baby-boom generation and therefore wants to get some other form of voluntary retirement scheme in place before phasing in the sad news.

These matters are best discussed in terms of numbers, however, so a small program to compute the value of an IRA in nominal dollars and constant dollars will be helpful.

PROGRAM 6E
IRA Accounts

```
10 PRINT "RATE=?, YRS=?"
15 INPUT IX
20 INPUT NY
25 PRINT IX; TAB 10;NY
30 PRINT "INFLATION=?"
35 INPUT F
40 PRINT F
50 LET Z=1+(IX−F)/100
60 LET T=2000*(1−Z↑NY)/(1−Z)
65 PRINT "ACCT.TOT.=$";T
```

The rate this program calls for as input is the annual yield on the IRA. The program assumes an annual contribution of $2,000.

Let's generate a table by running this program for an IRA yield of 10% and the inflation rates of 0%, 4%, 6%, and 8%, using thirty years as the calculation base. The program will give this information, suitably rounded off:

Inflation	Account total
0%	$328,988
4%	$158,116
6%	$112,170
8%	$ 81,136

If the inflation rate over the thirty years averages zero, you are in fine shape. You can pay yourself about $30,000 per year for at least eleven years (actually longer, since the balance in the account keeps earning interest). The problem starts with an inflation rate somewhere around 3% or so; it is worth noting that no administration has succeeded in keeping the rate this low for the last decade. The essence of the problem is that you are now paying your own retirement with inflated money (that was the nice part of Social Security—the withholding in current dollars was passed straight through that year in a form of self-indexing). If you pay yourself $30,000 for the year, you could wind up paying $7,000 in taxes (a guess from the 1982 tables), but the $23,000 that results from this is only going to be worth $7,800 in 1982 purchasing power in the 6% inflation case. This example is not chosen arbitrarily. It happens that earning interest at a rate about 4 or 5% above inflation is probably the best you are going to do; when the inflation rate is 0%, the banks just won't pay you 10%. For a truly horrifying example, put in 20% as your rate on the IRA against a background of 15% inflation. The government now sees you as rich folks (you have $2,363,763 in your account), but in fact you have just been getting by rather modestly (the real value is $132,878). So there is a punchline to this story and it is very simple. We will put this in big letters because it is critical:

The whole IRA plan hinges on either: (1) zero inflation, or (2) indexed income taxes over the life of the IRA. Point 1 won't happen. If anything goes wrong with Point 2, all bets are off.

The original indexing scheme proposed in the early 1980s has been under determined and persistent attack in Congress. There is ample historical precedent for the government deciding it needs a little more revenue and fiddling with the indexing provision. *Any* tampering with this will have serious impact on your IRA, if you have one.

On a more cheerful note, if you can contrive to die around age fifty-eight, having the money in an IRA will generally have lots of benefits for your dependents. Just don't count on doing so well yourself, unless the government shows unprecedented restraint during the next seven administrations.

So what can you do? One strategy is to use an IRA for investing in stocks or mutual funds in the hope that these will significantly outpace inflation. This kind of account will require a lot of attention and management, but it offers the prospect of better results than bank savings (and perhaps offers more risk, but this retirement business is a sporting proposition anyway). Another move that has some merit is using any extra money you may have to pay off a home loan early. At 12% on a thirty-year mortgage, every $1,000 you owe is costing you almost $4,000 over the years; you can reduce the principal on your home loan in most cases just by sending the $2,000 to the bank every year instead of into an IRA. Ask your loan officer for the details in this arrangement, but it is surprisingly effective. After all, the banks are lending all that IRA money back out as loans, and you may be sure they are charging more on the loans than they are paying on IRAs. The details of this proposition depend on your mortgage rate, the interest rate on accounts, and your tax situation, but as a crude estimate, if your mortgage is three percentage points higher than the interest rate, it starts to make sense.

Two conclusions really come out of this calculation, no matter what reasonable numbers are used. First, there is no surefire way to set aside money on paper during inflationary periods. This doesn't mean that you should go out and sink your funds into antique doilies or Krugerrands; it really means that you should try to begin thinking now of some sort of paying occupation you might like to pursue when you are older. Being able to earn current money is just about the only inflation hedge that is consistently worthwhile, and it isn't clear that either society or individuals benefit from the creation of a huge class of retirees. The second point is that you will probably have to find investments that pay better than bank interest. In this fascinating quest, the great thing is not to lose your shirt, and to this end you will find in the next chapter a short mathematical guide to the nature of speculation.

This area is a dark uncharted domain full of terrible pitfalls but generous rewards; if you have slogged through this book to this point, you may just be of a disposition to succeed in such endeavors.

7
Boom and Bust

If all the advice in this book is taken faithfully, and you succeed in minimizing your monthly payments on all fronts, you may then be confronted with a truly difficult problem: what can you do with surplus money that will enable you to get ahead? That is, what investment strategy is sufficiently defensive to protect your money and at the same time aggressive enough to allow you to hope to make some real gains?

There is absolutely no way for a book to recommend types of investment without appearing ridiculous at some time. Today's red-hot technology growth mutual fund becomes tomorrow's ill-managed dog; Chinese ceramics skyrocket one year and end up gathering dust at Grandma's the next. At the time this book is being written, diamonds, for example, have been one of the worst investments available. And yet diamonds may sparkle again someday.

But the computer can point out something rather profound, which is the similarity in the price history of all kinds of investments. The psychology of speculation can be examined rather closely in different computer models, and these models clarify the dynamics underlying all types of boom/bust cycles. These cycles have followed the same patterns for centuries, from grain speculation during wars in ancient times to the American stock market in the 1920s to the market for apartments in Atlanta in the 1970s.

"How Can You Lose?"

This question was posed to the author on a Saturday morning in the mid-1970s, in a real-estate office in Hermosa Beach, California. The reasoning behind it was that house prices in the overcooked little universe of Southern California beaches had for the previous year been climbing at a dizzying rate, approximately 40% per year. This had given rise to all sorts of speculative fever, and produced examples of financial paperwork that are not normally considered prudent banking practice.

At the heart of these schemes was the notion that the old rules of thumb in lending practice no longer applied to these cases. In the olden days (a period about four years earlier), it was thought to be a fairly risky business to take on monthly mortgage payments of more than 25% or so of one's monthly salary. This was based, more or less, on several decades of lending experience in gauging what payment level would be too tough to handle. The theory in this red-hot market, however, was that the going price of the house was going to rise enough per year to let the payments be made by a refinancing plan; under these circumstances, the income of the prospective borrower was practically irrelevant. After all, if the guy is buying a house for $60,000 now that will be worth $80,000 by Christmas, what could possibly be the problem? The payments are only going to be about ten grand for the whole year. How can you lose, right?

At this point, you may have already suspected from the rather cautious advice dispensed in previous chapters that the author of this work is an absolutely dreadful stick-in-the-mud and is going to proceed to dim the bright hopes of those golden days of yesteryear. If you think so, you are entirely correct. It is possible, with the aid of your redoubtable computer, to calculate the consequences of various statements that have been common in loose financial talk since the days when Roman grain dealers used to speculate on the Egyptian wheat crop. The conclusion from the various programs to be presented in this chapter will turn out to be fairly clear: when someone asks you

"How can you lose?" you should first check to make sure you still have your wallet with you, and then run screaming down the street as if a bear were chasing you.

It Doubles Every Six Months!

It is worthwhile to inspect the literal meaning of statements like this one. Here is a piece of program that follows the price course predicted above:

```
10 PRINT "START PRICE=?"
20 INPUT P
25 PRINT "NEW PRICE IS . . ."
30 FOR K=1 TO 16
40 LET P=P*2
50 PRINT "$";P,6*K;"MOS"
60 NEXT K
```

To give this a little flavor, we will say that the starting price is $100 for a colonial pewter goblet, during a year when Americana is enjoying a boom. RUN the program and you should see the following output:

```
NEW PRICE IS . . .
$200          6MOS
$400          12MOS
$800          18MOS
$1600         24MOS
$3200         30MOS
$6400         36MOS
$12800        42MOS
$25600        48MOS
$51200        54MOS
$102400       60MOS
$204800       66MOS
$409600       72MOS
$819200       78MOS
$1638400      84MOS
$3276800      90MOS
$6553600      96MOS
```

So what is going on here is that, as you step out into the bright sunlight outside the auction holding a genuine colonial pewter goblet, for which you have paid $100, the expectation that antiques of this type double every six months means the expectation that someone will be happy to give you more than *six million dollars for it six years later!* What a deal!

In fact, there have been periods in which prices of certain antiques doubled in six months. There have been times in which particular stock prices doubled in one day. Empty lots in Florida have from time to time doubled in a month. But what the program above suggests is that this process is exceedingly unlikely to last for many months or even years. In the case of the pewter goblet, there are probably other things one could do with six million dollars to amuse oneself other than gloat over an old mug; in the case of articles that are more expensive to start with, e.g., a $10,000 diamond, the final price after a healthy growth period, say, thirty years, would equal the entire GNP of the United States in constant 1982 dollars.

This type of growth curve, which is called exponential growth, is for reasons that are lost in the odd wiring of the human nervous system almost always projected at the outset of any speculation. The reasoning on paper is clean enough, and actually it follows the same lines as the idea of compound interest. The problem that arises to foil these projections has three sources, which will be examined, in detail, in a fancier price model later in this chapter. Briefly, they are (1) the price of everything is linked to everything else (it's hard to charge $1000 for an orange when tangerines are 30¢); (2) there is only so much money available for speculation, and (3) sooner or later people get nervous and begin selling whatever they have that has shot up in price.

"How Can You Lose?" Continued

Somehow doubling may seem like an extreme example, so it can be toned down to a smaller rate of increase in the interests of plausibility. In fact, we may as well type in a general price-increase program and use the numbers for the real-estate situation described at the beginning of the chapter. Not to spoil an interesting punch line, but it will turn out that *no* constant factor increase can possibly be sustained for very long (and when it is no longer sustained, watch out!). Here is the program listing:

PROGRAM 7A
Exponential Growth

```
10 PRINT "START PRICE=?"
15 INPUT P
20 PRINT P
25 PRINT "PERCENT INCREASE=?"
30 INPUT Z
35 PRINT Z;" PERCENT"
40 LET Z=Z/100
45 FOR K=1 TO 15
50 LET P=P*(1+Z)
55 LET PT=INT(P)
60 LET P$=STR$(PT)
65 PRINT K;TAB(12−LEN(P$));PT
70 NEXT K
```

This program has a little bit of fancy output formatting in lines 55, 60, and 65; it makes the price column printed by the program come out neatly (this use of string functions in programming is covered nicely in most computer manuals). This is meant as an encouragement to consult your manual to find out how to do pretty output. If you don't feel like doing this, just scrap lines 55 and 60 and change 65 to

```
65 PRINT K,P
```

The case to try here is the beach house, starting at $45,000, at the real-estate agent's sure-thing, can't-miss, practically guaranteed rate of increase, 40%. ENTER these when you RUN the program and you get:

1	63000
2	88200
3	123480
4	172872
5	242020
6	338829
7	474360
8	664105
9	929747
10	1301645
11	1822304
12	2551226
13	3571716
14	5000403
15	7000564

If, and of course this is an *if* of truly monumental proportions, the property could actually increase at the projected rate, many miracles would be possible. For example, it would be possible to make all the payments on the house by refinancing every year; just take the $18,000 price increase between the start and year one and compare it to the payments, which would have been running about $6,000 per year. Even if all sorts of creative financing had to be invoked (separate loans for the down payment, for example), raising the payments to $10,000 per year in the short term, how could this be a problem in light of the spectacular increase in property value?

Well, the problem may be briefly stated by noting that the house now sells for about $95,000 rather than the one million bucks indicated in the table. It peaked at the fairly dizzy price of $120,000 at the height of the boom and was at one point changing hands every six months or so. A cynic might observe that, even in 1983, a million dollars would have been considered pretty expensive for a tiny cottage with leaky plumbing. The real price of this house adjusted for inflation over the ten-year period of interest is about $59,000 in constant dollars, which is a real increase, but not especially spectacular for a decade. It's probably all for the best; it's not clear

who would have been able to handle the $17,000-per-
month payments (projected for 1983) in a neighborhood
clogged with unemployed stewardesses.

Boom and Bust: A General Model

The pattern of prices during a speculative fever has tended,
historically, to follow the same tragicomic course since
ancient times. Speculation in basic foodstuffs was epi-
demic in the societies of the ancient Mediterranean, and
in fact a great deal of energy was expended by early gov-
ernments to prevent mob violence by keeping grain prices
stable. The reason that price increases could not go on
indefinitely in ancient economies was fairly simple: since
the money was real money, typically precious metal coin-
age, the price of all available grain could rapidly approach
the value of all available money. In practice, the government would break down and people would begin murder-
ing the speculators before the money supply was con-
sumed. This circumstance is perhaps a little harsh, but
there is not much evidence that it served to discourage
speculation.

The truly classic example of speculation, closer to
modern times but still remote enough to be quaint, is the
"tulip fever" that seized Holland shortly after the arrival
there of tulip bulbs from Turkey in the early seventeenth
century. Fancy varieties of tulips (striped, odd colors, etc.)
began to appear, and the price of tulip-bulb novelties began
to climb rapidly. Particular single bulbs, at the height of
the frenzy, were selling for the equivalent of a house in
Amsterdam. When the market collapsed, and tulips began
to sell for the price of a flower, thousands of speculators
were left with nothing to do with their expensive bulbs,
except perhaps eat them (after all, they're more or less
like onions).

There are several conclusions one may draw from
this curio from the dawn of true capitalism. One point
might be, "Gee, those Dutch guys must have been nuts!"
Another possible conclusion might be, "Hey, no way I'll

ever pay more than \$500 for a flower!" These sentiments, while correct as far as they go, can be expanded by looking into the reason that someone would trade his house for a tulip bulb. It is also worth keeping in mind the trivial observation that someone is on both the selling and the buying end of every stock transaction, and that millions of living Americans, as opposed to long-gone Hollanders, have managed to buy stocks as overpriced as striped tulips once were.

The reason prices go up is that people think they will go up. People buy the article in question and are willing to pay a little more for it, since they think it will be worth more soon anyway. This process continues until the first serious wavering in price, at which some owners of the article panic and begin selling, which then drives the price down rapidly. The point at which the price of a speculative article continues to increase, *but at a noticeably slower rate*, becomes a truly dangerous point; many people holding the article are doing so in expectation of a particular return, and when the return falters and their brother-in-law needs his money back for some reason or a further payment is required, the result is absolute chaos. After the crash, prices tend to settle around their true exchange value with the speculative component factored out. That's why house prices never crash quite as badly as the price of empty lots.

The rules of this game, for the purposes of formulating a programming model, may be summarized in two principles that will translate directly into statements in BASIC. The principles are:

The limits of money   A given article can rise in price very rapidly at the outset of speculation, but as the price passes a certain point, the amount of money available for further price increases starts decreasing. This occurs partly because the number of speculators and the amount of money they can raise is limited, and partly because there is no article for which some sort of substitute cannot be found. Even in the stock market of the 1920s, the number of possible new entrants to the game finally dried up. During the gold boom circa 1980, the electronics industry and other major consumers of gold began finding, with amazing speed, ways to avoid using it. The key point is not how far away the limits are at the start of a boom, but that there are eventual limits.

The limits of confidence Just as the price increases during a boom are fueled by the expectation of further increases, very sharp, in fact uncontrollable, price drops can occur once this confidence is damaged. The subtle point is not that people need to anticipate prices going down for the boom to collapse, but rather that all that needs to happen is that they anticipate that price increases will slow down. And the mechanism for this slowdown is the limitation on the amount of money available for further increases. A model for this effect simply takes into account a factor in which people's opinion of the next round of prices is based on the last round of price changes.

The idea here is to replace the expression for price increases that has been used in the inflation models so far, namely:

NEWPRICE = OLDPRICE * CONSTANT

where CONSTANT is a number such as 2 or 1.40, with a new expression:

NEWPRICE = OLDPRICE * OPTIMISM * POSSIBILITY

where optimism is a factor that predicts a confidence level in further price increases, and possibility is a factor that takes into account the limits on money supply and number of speculators.

The following program is an attempt to make a simple but realistic model along these lines. This first version of it takes a little more than 1K RAM on most computers, but there are hints to follow for shrinking the program if you have a really tiny workspace (e.g., stock VIC 20 or Sinclair ZX81). First we will list the program and consider some sample outputs.

PROGRAM 7B
Boom/Bust

```
10 PRINT "INPUT P,PNEW"
15 INPUT P
20 INPUT PNEW
25 LET SIZE=100*P
30 FOR K=1 TO 20
35 LET OP=1+3.14*(PNEW−P)/P
40 IF OP<=0 THEN GOTO 110
45 LET POSS=(SIZE−3*PNEW)/SIZE
50 LET POSS=POSS↑0.3
55 LET POLD=PNEW
60 LET PNEW=P*OP*POSS
65 LET PX=.01*INT(POSS*100)
70 LET P=POLD
75 LET OX=.01*INT(OP*100)
80 PRINT INT (PNEW);TAB (10);OX;" ";PX
85 NEXT K
90 GOTO 120
110 PRINT "BUST****"
120 STOP
```

To run this in a smaller amount of memory, delete lines 10, 15, 20, 65, and 75, and enter the new output line:

80 PRINT PNEW,OP

The output won't be identical to that of the longer program but will give the same numerical results. The program then must be given values for P and PNEW before it is run. This is done by using LET statements with no line number to assign P and PNEW outside the program.)

Let's do two trial runs of this program before really looking at the mechanics of it. Here is a first sample with a market that takes off fast. INPUT the values 100 for P and 130 for PNEW.

191	1.94	0.98
318	2.49	0.98
572	3.07	0.97
1053	3.5	0.94

1860	3.64	0.89
2806	3.4	0.78
2778	2.59	0.57
1587	0.96	0.58

BUST****

The first column tracks the price level for our article (a hot stock would be a good example), the second column traces the optimism level, and the third column reflects the quantity POSS for possibility. The sinister thing to note on the way to the final drop is that the optimism column can actually start falling before the prices drop; in fact, the model is probably reflecting more accurately the attitude of really shrewd speculators who are watching the amount of price changes rather than just the price level. In this run, the point at which the price hits 1860 is where the smart money is cashing in (after all, if you got in on the deal at 318 you're rolling in profit) and the suckers are crowding in on the last few days of glory. This model just ends in BUST**** when optimism goes negative, because under these conditions no price computation is really possible; after the stock market was seen to be crashing in October 1929, it was impossible for brokers to establish any price at all for the stocks of countless fine old American firms.

Let's try something with a slower start: this time INPUT 100 for P and 103 for PNEW. The output now looks like:

108	1.09	0.99
118	1.16	0.99
139	1.3	0.98
181	1.54	0.98
266	1.94	0.98
437	2.47	0.97
769	3.01	0.95
1369	3.38	0.92
2263	3.44	0.85
2969	3.04	0.71
2305	1.98	0.51
620	0.29	0.7

BUST****

Although this particular case takes a little longer to get wound up to fever pitch, once it gets hot it finally peaks and crashes at roughly the same rate as the earlier example. Note that from price level 266 there are four rounds in which the price approximately doubles, guaranteeing that when you are offered an opportunity to get in on this swinging deal at 2969, someone is sure to ask you, "How can you lose?"

Some features of this model you might want to tinker with in the interests of melodrama or realism are:

"Nervousness" This model uses the number 3.14 in the line that defines the variable OP. If you use a bigger number here the market acts jumpier, and if you use a smaller number the market acts more sluggish.

Market size The money pool available for speculation is here projected to be fairly small (the variable SIZE, which is used to define POSS). This is mostly to fit a reasonable run on one pass through your display screen. With a bigger value for SIZE, the program can churn away for a long time.

For computer users who have a nice chunk of RAM available (16K or so), one really interesting possibility is to do lots of output scrolling and introduce a random component to prices by using the random number function built into most versions of BASIC. It may be the case that a great many speculations are brought down by people's reaction to the inevitable fluctuations, sometimes large and downwards, which occur as a result of the buy/sell decisions in the market being made by large numbers of unrelated individuals.

For advanced thinkers who would like to see the effect of a little randomness in investor psychology, here is a line to add to the program that will put some excitement in the output. Type in

```
37 LET OP=OP+0.2*(1−RND(1))*OP
```

On most computers, RND will pop up a number between 0 and 1 every time it is called. Please look up RND(x) in your computer manual and check two points: first, whether you have to call another function such as

RAND or RND(−TI) to initialize the sequence of random numbers; and second, whether you have to call RND(1) or can just use RND with no dummy value in parentheses. This is another encouragement to check your manual; most of these are more informative than the typical college programming class anyway.

Here the possible size of fluctuation in optimism is scaled to the amount of optimism itself, which is fairly reasonable. Strictly speaking, this should probably be scaled to the square root of OP instead, but the reasons for this are somewhat complex. It would also be interesting to start the model with a larger quantity for SIZE and also subject this to random fluctuations; that, in fact, is exactly the way large quantities in money markets behave.

One of the reasons that people still buy stocks (and bet on horses, for that matter) is that it requires rather a keen judgment to determine when a price has been subjected to a setback as a result of a momentary fluctuation and when a price has taken a drop as a result of the "end of the line" having drawn near. Guessing this choice right or wrong is probably the source of more family comedies or tragedies than even such advanced topics as lust or jealousy.

Now run the same program three or four times with the addition of line 37 (or lines 36 and 37, if you have to call an initialization in your version of BASIC). You will see that sometimes the fluctuations set off really explosive booms and sometimes they cause them to fizzle out fairly early. If you change the factor in line 37 from 0.2 to 0.8 or so, you can induce some really strange behavior. This example, probably more than any of the others in this book, suggests what a remarkable power is now available to everyone with a home computer and a few free hours. With some tinkering with values in this program, it is possible to model all sorts of economic matters that were reserved for specialists only a decade ago. Perhaps part of the value of the widespread availability of computers will be an increasing unwillingness on the part of many people to "take the specialist's word for it." Keep an eye on your money, and take nothing on faith!

8
Conclusions

If there is one solid conclusion from all the chapters in this book, it is this:

"Easy payments" are easy for the lender. They cost you much more in the long run.

It's just about an iron law of economics that you are never going to get rich if you have lots of debt financed at 20% and are paying it off with the smallest possible payments. There are lots of things you can do without; if you want to buy lots of goods on time, the thing you will be doing without is money.

Here is another conclusion:

It is practically impossible for people to be "numerical" about money. That's why you need a computer.

Think about this situation. (*Really* think about it—if you get this straight, this book will have saved you thousands of dollars.) You are sitting in a bank on one of those momentous occasions when you are refinancing a house. The way this works is that the loan will go off at whatever the interest rate is at the time you sign on the deal. After a few days of hassling, you are finally walking towards your bank, about to sign papers on $60,000 at 12.5%, when you notice that the bank across the street is offering 12.25%. Is it worth the trouble of starting all that paperwork all over again?

This is what is meant by needing a computer: you almost certainly can't make yourself feel that ¼% is a big deal. The computer will tell you in this case that it's worth $4,180 over the life of the loan. As you stand in front of the bank, think this over: you can make up this $4,000 by denying yourself small things for decades, or you can walk across the street and get the better rate.

In a more pointed example, suppose the home loan rate is 11.5% and your paperwork was done up last year at 12.75%. Even so, it's hard to make yourself feel that this is so dramatic. The computer will be happy to tell you that the difference between a $60,000 loan on these two rates is $20,860 over the loan term. Or in other terms, about $50 a month, every month, year after year. You can save that $50 every month by wearing the same old socks with holes in them instead of buying new ones, or spending $600 less on Christmas every year, or never taking a vacation, or comparison-shopping brands of hot dogs. Or you can walk into a bank and rewrite your loan. Take your pick! Either scrimp for decades or spend a few hours with the nasty old bankers. You can be sure that if you just sit on your expensive paperwork, which is what most people do, the bankers will love you.

The same conclusion applies to car loans and credit-card purchases as well. You can't eat interest, and it won't keep you warm at night, but it is what you're buying with your paycheck. Every chance to pay off loans at high rates should be taken in preference to saving; i.e., don't owe money at 20% and lend it to the bank at 5.25%. If you have some sudden emergency, you can probably charge it on the same old credit cards you just paid off anyway, so you probably don't need a fictitious cash reserve.

In all these cases you can use your computer to state your choices in a forceful way. Look at the numbers that result from different deals and ask yourself, "is it easier for me to save money by paying less interest or by eating peanut-butter sandwiches for lunch every day for a year?" Pull that game software off your computer and start playing for money!

If you get interested in programming, you should consult some of the excellent books on BASIC available these days, preferably those issued by Addison-Wesley (such as

BASIC and the Personal Computer by Dwyer and Critch-field, or *Using BASIC on the IBM PC* by the Trombettas.) You may find that as you get out from under some of your payments you have time for more intellectual adventures, and the adventure represented by programming is one of the most interesting ever offered to the general public. Take care, keep thinking, and don't give your money away.

APPENDIX

This Book
and Your Computer

The programs for this book were written in a dialect of BASIC that is a subset of the standard small-computer BASIC developed by Microsoft. They have been run on Apples, IBM PCs, Osbornes, Kaypros, and many other mid-sized machines exactly as written here.

The only points to watch are:

- Find out what the exponent operator is on your keyboard. We have used ↑ here because it is the most common, but ∧ and ** also turn up.
- Some displays leave a lot of earlier material on the screen and some don't. You may find you have to clear the screen yourself between runs.
- The programs were written with a 32-column display in mind. Most will work even at 22 columns, but if you have trouble with odd line divisions, just put part of the offending PRINT statement on the next line. For example, a line like

```
10 PRINT A;TAB(10);B
```

can just as well be

```
10 PRINT A
12 PRINT B
```

if necessary.

This book went through a test phase in which maniacs with nine-year-old Altairs and Exidy Sorcerers and every other odd box tried to find program hang-ups. There was nothing that couldn't be adapted with a single line change, so be confident that it will work for you no matter what.

Atari 400/800 and Newer Models

Fortunately for you, Atari BASIC is virtually devoid of tricks. There are now even some convenience features that would allow you to make programs more compact. The RND(N) function in the programs of chapter 7 requires an argument but is pre-initialized for you (look this up in your manual or in the very nice book *Atari BASIC* by Albrecht, Finkel, and Brown, published by Wiley). Your display has enough columns that all the output of the programs will fit with no modification. In fact, the only reason we are putting in this note about Atari is that technically, Atari BASIC is different in some ways from the standard; it's just that none of the nonstandard features are called for in this humble work.

VIC 20/Commodore 64

You don't even have to go through your copy of the book and change all the ↑ symbols to ∧. For the C64 you are now just about home free. The only problem you may have is that the superior display capabilities of your machine roll lists past you faster than you can see them. You might want, on both the VIC 20 and C64, to change line 30 in the program Boom/Bust (chapter 7) to:

```
30 FOR K=D TO D+10
```

Run the program the first time by setting D=1 with a LET statement before entering RUN. Then get the next batch of lines with:

```
LET D=12
GOTO 30
```

This way you can step through the program and follow its course on the screen. Believe it or not, some machines have such slow display routines that you can watch the lines come out one at a time. That doesn't make life easy for games designers.

The VIC 20 is a wonderful computer value but for

historical reasons has only a 22-column screen. When you encounter an output line that breaks awkwardly, just split it. For example, in Program 5C on mortgages, the line

```
120 PRINT "CHANGE? AM=1,RT=2,YRS=3,NO=4"
```

can just be changed to

```
120 PRINT "CHANGE? AM=1,RT=2"
121 PRINT "YRS=3,NO=4"
```

You may console yourself for the extra labor with two thoughts. First, the VIC and C64 keyboards are in many ways the nicest to use for both comfort and convenience (you do a minimum of shifting). Second, you get your answers back in milliseconds instead of seconds. As an added bonus, you get rather polite error messages. The only remaining point to note is that in chapter 7 you should remember to initialize your random-number routines with a statement like:

```
2 LET Y=RND(−TI)
```

See your manual for the reason for this.

Timex/Sinclair 1000/1500/2068

These programs were developed and run on a Sinclair ZX/81, so all you will have to do is:

- Go back and replace all the ↑ symbols with ∗∗. For the Timex 2068 (or Spectrum), you don't even have to do this, since the keyboard has been changed.
- Take out the ( ) in expressions with TAB, i.e., TAB 10 instead of TAB(10).

You will note as you type in the programs that the line breaks occur exactly as they do on your screen; that's because the 32-column screen has been used here as standard. The Timex is the author's favorite computer. After fulminating against rip-offs by credit-card companies and banks, it's hard to feel really positive about the pricing policies of Apple and IBM, whatever one thinks about their hardware.

Texas Instruments TI 99/4A

TI BASIC has some nice features you may want to use to modify the programs. If not, just take them as they are: all the output fits on a 32-column screen, the exponent operator is ↑ just as shown, and you have more than enough memory and processor speed (there are a few programs here in which having a real 16-bit machine makes things nicer, so you can chuckle at the plodders with their 6502s and Z80s).

Some points to consider:

• TI has a nice input format. You can do

```
10 INPUT "AMT=":A
```

instead of

```
10 PRINT "AMT="
15 INPUT A
```

the way most of the programs in this book are written.

• You might want to put something like this:

```
5 CALL CLEAR
```

to clean up the screen at the beginning of each program.

• In chapter 7, there are programs with calls to the random function RND. You should put a line

```
2 RANDOMIZE
```

in the top of each program for truly random results.

If you bought your TI for $149 or so, you are to be congratulated for your astuteness, and if you paid more, you are at least a pioneer. The author hopes this book will be one of your most useful low-cost peripherals.

Radio Shack TRS-80 Model I, III

It is probably the case that these programs will run on everything from a PC-1 to a Model II, but they have specifically been checked out on these two workhorses. All you have to do is change all the ↑ symbols to ∧ and you are ready to go. The space requirements are absolutely minimal (a 4K original Model I is practically overkill), and the format considerations are the same (same INPUT type, column-size of the screen is sufficient). If you see your display for some strange reason racing in chapter 7, just check out the hint given in the section on VIC 20s. There are lots of really nice books of programs for TRS-80 models (the one by Charles Sternberg is a good example, and available at Radio Shack stores). In a way, this book grew out of a desire to extend the usefulness of the standard "mortgage and checkbook" programs to focus on the critical issues of interest, inflation, and taxes.

INDEX
BASIC Examples and BASIC Programs

Other books in the Microcomputer Books Series, available from your local computer store or bookstore. For more information write:

General Publishing Group
Addison-Wesley Publishing Company, Inc.
Reading, Massachusetts 01867
(617) 944-3700

5110

10286   **The Addison-Wesley
Book of Atari Software
1984**
J. Stanton, R. Wells,
S. Rochowansky, and
M. Mellin

10285   **The Addison-Wesley
Book of Apple Software
1984**
J. Stanton, R. Wells,
S. Rochowansky, and
M. Mellin

06896   **The IBM Personal
Computer From the
Inside Out**
Murray Sargent III and
Richard Shoemaker

05208   **The Netweaver's
Sourcebook: A Guide to
Micro Networking and
Communications**
Dean Gengle